ISBN-9781515223665
Printed in the United States of America
First Printing 2015

To Leslie and Hank —

This is the book book I published —
It features my mother's recipes (which were
not very good) and a bunch of family stories
(mostly true.) It was written with humor

The Wonderful World of Food

and love. I hope you enjoy it.

Becky

Beyond the City Limits
of Waukegan, Illinois

An Edwards Family Cookbook

Becky Yasenchak

by Becky Edwards Yasenchak

Acknowledgments

I have received a great deal of encouragement and assistance in compiling and completing this cookbook. My sisters, Sharon and Kathy helped me with the family stories. Our son Dave offered criticism. Our daughter Ronda had a duel role serving as my personal computer specialist and providing critical recipe-review checking for clarity as well as accuracy.

My Monday afternoon writing group listened to countless stories and always asked for more. A good friend, DeeAnn Bogue, proofed my recipes and uncovered many errors. Debbie Martin is my writing buddy. She reformatted the entire text. Thanks to Deb, the recipes are clearer and easier to follow.

My husband, Ron has provided constant support and patience. This book would not exist without his help. For the past seven years, Ron and I have lived at our beach home on the central Oregon coast. Geographically, politically, and socially it's about as far away as one can get beyond the city limits of Waukegan Illinois.

In 1970 we moved to Portland and I discovered whole new food groups I never knew existed. I also discovered the joys of wine. My guide was *THE COMPLETE WINE AND FOOD COOKBOOK* by Dr. Harold C. Torbert. Dr. Torbert was an American doctor living in Paris. Until I purchased this book I'd never considered cooking with wine, or drinking a glass of wine with dinner. His beef tenderloin recipe on page 23 started it all. Thank you, Dr. Torbert. My copy of his book is 45 years old. It is tattered and battered, and numerous pages are stained with remnants of one or more ingredients. I treasure the book.

There are snippets and stories scattered throughout this book, but it is primarily a cookbook with real recipes, old and new. Most of the recipes have survived a history of being modified, substituted, and/or screwed up in one way or another. In spite of the flagrant lack of attention to detail, most turned out pretty well. At this point all of the recipes have been tested for validity and accuracy. This recipe collection is given with humor and with love.

Enjoy, and get cooking!
Becky Edwards Yasenchak
July 2015

Foreword: About Me, My Life, and Food...

Beyond the City Limits shares my favorite recipes for my favorite foods. In addition to recipes, the book includes anecdotes and stories from my family and our life in Waukegan, Illinois.

Our home on South Butrick Street was filled with kids, chaos, chores, bickering, laughter, and love. Most of my early memories are tied to our kitchen and the meals we shared in that time and place. Almost every chapter begins with a family memory and one or more of my mother's recipes. Some of her recipes are good; others are dreadful.

I leave it to you the reader/cook to draw your own conclusions. In Mom's defense she did an admirable job considering the constraints she faced and the options she was given. My goal is to contrast the meals and foods I knew as a child to the menu choices and options we have today.

Inside the City Limits of Waukegan – 1943 to 1964 As I remember it...

Waukegan is a small industrial city located on the shores of Lake Michigan roughly half way between Chicago and Milwaukee. Most of my memories are from the 1950's.

The quiet neighborhoods had tree-lined streets with single-family homes that were stick-built, well maintained, and rarely locked. Most homes had big porches facing the street and a single detached garage accessed either by a driveway or a network of alleys. We lived in a two-story craftman's style house built in 1911. My parents bought our house in 1945 for $6,000. It had a thirty-year mortgage. Dad was convinced he paid too much.

Our neighbors were mostly first and second generation Americans from Western Europe; Germany, Poland, Italy, Austria, Armenia, Yugoslavia, and Greece. The men worked in the local factories and the women stayed at home. The families all had children. Many were close to my age and we played together.

Their mothers baked incredible breads, pastries, and desserts. I was invited to stay for dinner on several occasions, but I always declined. I was expected at home. Besides, they ate weird food. My family was 100% American. I ate All-American food twice a day, every day, with a few notable exceptions:

French Dressing: See salads

French Fried Potatoes: We all liked fries and had a French-fry cooker filled with oil. Every now and then Mom would discard the old oil and replace it.

French Toast: Mom made this when we were long on stale bread and short on eggs. The bread was dipped into a mixture of eggs and milk, and then pan fried in bacon grease. It was served with Log Cabin Syrup® that was packaged in a little log cabin.

German Chocolate Cake: Mom made this from scratch. I do not have her recipe.

Italian Spaghetti: We had this once a week. See pasta

Spanish Rice: A can of Spanish rice and a pound hamburger meat fed our family.

Swedish Meatballs: Mom made these and smaller Salisbury steaks with hamburger, breadcrumbs and an egg. A can of mushroom soup set them apart.In the 1950's the big war was over and we'd won. I was told America was the strongest, bravest, and best country in the world, and I believed it. We lived in a democracy where rulers were chosen and the people had the right to disagree and express their beliefs and opinions.

Democracy had no place in our household. Dad reigned supreme. As children we lived in chaotic harmony with our family despot. He had rules about eating, talking back, school work, chores, church, manners, and cleanliness. We understood Dad was always right, even when he was dead wrong, and we challenged him at our personal peril.

Mom had learned to cook from her mother who had cooked in a logging camp. In the days before Julia Child exposed the Art of French Cooking, Mom was considered a good cook. I don't remember any cook books, but she had a small notebook where she kept *special* recipes she'd acquired from friends. I treasure that notebook today.

Our home-cooked meals were hot, passable, and predictable. They were duplications of the same fare served throughout the midwest. Supper was served when Dad came home from work. Late-comers did not eat. Our family sat at the kitchen table in assigned seats. We always said grace. Then Mom put food on our plates and we were expected to eat it. No talking was allowed, except for Dad, and sometimes Mom. We couldn't reach for food, bicker, snicker, or squirm. And God help anyone who dropped something on the floor or spilled their milk.

I enjoyed Mom's meals back then, but I don't eat that way today; I can't. My sedentary life-style coupled with my genetic propensity for heart disease and diabetes has forced me to make healthier food choices. After decades of steaming fresh vegetables, and sauteing with olive oil I have (almost) convinced myself that fried foods are not very tasty. Fortunately, there's a wide range of flavorful substitutes to help ease the withdrawal from gravies, breading, fat, and salt.

In 1962 I left Waukegan and attended a college far beyond the city limits. I was exposed to new ideas, different social concepts, and completely different, exciting food choices. In retrospect, I seriously doubt that dormitory food and the local college restaurants were superior in any way to Mom's cooking. It was different. I ate new things that may have existed somewhere in Waukegan, but never appeared at my family home. In time I left college and lived in several different places. I bought a cookbook, and then another. I started and continued to expand my cooking knowledge and experience.

I faithfully watched Julia Child and other chefs; I experimented with seafood, shellfish, poultry, pastas, rices, and soups. Purchasing *fresh* fruits and vegetables, herbs and spices. I searched for recipes that embraced different cultures, customs and pallets. Over the years I purchased countless cookbooks and saved boxes of recipes. Given my obsession with food, it was only a matter of time before I attempted to write a cookbook.

Beyond the City Limits has been a work in process, and it's almost had a life of its own. In the beginning, I found a blank cookbook and filled it with recipes from my kitchen. I gave it, and a set of decent pots and pans to our son when he married. Dave thanked me. Our daughter Ronda, had been after me for years to put together a family cookbook. When I finally made one, and gave it to *David*...she was hurt and offended.

I apologized and made a cookbook for her that was an expanded, far better version of David's book. I added a lot of recipes and I included stories and insights about my family and our life in Waukegan. I called the book <u>Leaving Little Fort.</u> Ronda loved it, and almost forgave me for letting David come first. Then other people wanted a cookbook; so did I. I bought a computer and started typing.

That was about sixteen years ago. At one point I had almost completed the cookbook when I found a special class for *"Cooks and Would Be Cook Book Writers."* To my husband's chagrin I took the class and began revising and correcting the recipes. Since then there have been countless reincarnations. In retrospect I realized I had to *leave* the city limits of Waukegan to learn about food. I also had to mature a little before I could master cooking. I changed the name of the cookbook from *Leaving Littlefort* to *Beyond the City Limits.*

My husband Ron has witnessed this odyssey from the beginning. He provided a few recipes, critical support, and much needed editing. After well more than a decade he is pretty tired of the whole cookbook project. Occasionally I'm forced to remind him that it was his idea to share this effort with others. It is a family history, and perhaps it'll provide some insight into why Larry, Sharon, Kathy, and I turned out the way we did.

The collection of family stories and recipes is dedicated to my mother, Mabel Aldridge Edwards Peasley. Mom had a wonderful, upbeat disposition. She could and frequently did laugh at anything…especially herself. She was always willing and frequently eager to help others.

At a time when most women stayed at home, Mom worked full time as a registered nurse. Dad convinced her to work 11pm to 7am so she could be home during the day to clean the house, shop, cook, and care for her husband and four children.

Mom was also the family nurse. If anyone in the family needed special nursing care, they would call Mom. She would drop everything and nurse them back to health. I had a life-changing accident when I was eleven-months old. I needed almost constant care for several months. Mom was my nurse. She was a truly remarkable woman.

When we moved to Oregon I discovered whole food groups I did not know existed. I experimented, took classes, and little by little I became a cook. *Beyond the City Limits* is my attempt to share the truly great hits, as well as the disasters. I don't cook like my mother did. I have scores of cookbooks, years of experience, almost endless options, and plenty of latitude. However, I think I would chuck all of it if I could sit at my Mom's table, surrounded by my family, one more time.

Mom moved from Tucson to Portland in 1993. Sharon and I settled her into an assisted-living retirement home. She spent many weekends with Ron and I. Mom thought I was a great cook because I fixed something special whenever she stayed. She thought Ron was a prince because he was very good to her and he put up with me.

Mom's been gone almost sixteen years. Every time I think of her, I think of food. She enjoyed a good cup of coffee and she absolutely loved to eat. In a sharp contrast she *hated* extra pounds. Mom would eat, gain weight, and then she would diet, exercise, and eat some more. She successfully fought her weight battle for all but the last years of her life.

This collection of recipes and stories is dedicated to her.

Part I – The Main Ingredients

Chapter 1 - Beef:

In my house, everyone ate meat every day. When we talked about MEAT.. We were generally referring to BEEF, the meat of choice. *Inside* Waukegan's City Limits it would be *un-American* to not like beef.

Chapter 2 - Pork:

Pork used to be a four-letter word meaning fat. At my house, all pork products were marbled and layered in fat. Pigs had a better chance at sprouting wings and flying than ever becoming lean, 'Pork Fat Ruled.' I grew up with metaphors like: Pig Out, Bring Home the Bacon, and Fat as a Pig. The Chinese discovered pork eons ago and they use every part of a pig but the pig's sweat and squeal!

Chapter 3 – Fried Chicken:

Back then chickens were sold whole. My mom cut up and fried chicken once a week. Today, chickens are a huge commercial business. They may never fly, but they sure get around.

Chapter 4 – Turkey:

Turkeys are versatile, large birds that never could fly. We had turkey *once* a year, on Thanksgiving. The turkey was usually cooked too long. The meat was dry. Fortunately there was plenty of gravy to help it along and lots of other stuff eat. It really didn't matter.

Chapter 5 - Other Feathered Fowl

There are other less common feathered fowl that are commercially available: These include Cornish Hens, duck, goose and pheasant. Some game birds are available only to the families of intrepid hunters.

Part II: Food Served Before, With, and After a Main Meal

1. REAL MEAT, BEEF

Several years ago one of the fast-food restaurant chains ran an ad that featured an outspoken, elderly woman. She was holding the two halves of a hamburger and demanding "Where's the Beef?" I felt like I was back in Waukegan.

In the 1950's everyone that I knew ate meat every day and the meat of choice was beef. At our house beef was pretty much limited to three cuts: ground beef, pot roast, and steak. About once a week we would have pot roast with onions, carrots and potatoes. Our every-day beef meals usually began with ground beef. Mom could feed her family of six with 1½ pounds of what we called hamburger meat. A few years later 'Hamburger Helper'© capitalized on many of the ground beef concoctions that were popular in the 1950's. These were some of Mom's specialties:

Meatloaf: Mom made a good meatloaf. In contrast, all of my meatloaf attempts have fallen short. I don't have Mom's recipe. I tried to get it, but when I asked about specific ingredients, or how much to use, mom's responses were vague references that generally started with 'some'. I remember Mom mixed the meatloaf with her bare hands and based the correct amounts on the way it felt. I think her success with meatloaf as well as life had a lot to do with knowing how much was enough. After years or trying, I have given up ever making a perfect or even passable meatloaf.

Pot Roast with Pan Gravy: We had beef pot roast maybe twice a month and it was a real treat. Mom would use a large, two to three pound blade-cut chuck roast. She floured the roast and browned it in bacon grease over high heat. Then she lowered the heat, added liquid and lots of root vegetables. The finished pot roast was fork-tender and more than enough food for a single meal. My dad was entitled to any and all leftovers.

Steaks

Salisbury Steaks: These steaks were something Mom made when she didn't have time for meatloaf. She mixed ground beef with an egg, added salt and dry onion soup. The meat was formed into little steaks and pan fried them until it was no longer pink.

Cube Steaks: I believe these 'steaks' are made from a less-tender cut of chuck roast. The butcher would slice a small slab of meat about 3/8 of an inch thick. Then he'd run it through a tenderizer that pulverized it. He'd turn the meat over and repeat the process, again, and again. With each pass, the slab of meat would get thinner and bigger. These steaks were cooked quickly over high heat. I think they're still available. It would make sense that a chunk of beef prepared in that manner should be tender. I think they were chewy. Very chewy.

When my (rich) Aunt Sophia and Uncle Ray came they would buy steak for all of us. I don't know how Mom cooked it, but the adults considered it a treat. I only got a small piece. I didn't really like it, so I didn't care. I think I was at least fourteen years old before I realized that hamburger and steak came from the same animal. I was a lot older before I learned how to prepare beef correctly.

The rest of the beef recipes are mine. Some of them I made up, some I found in cookbooks or borrowed from friends. The rest I simply stole fair and square. The recipes are divided into 4 different categories: Ground Beef, Steaks, Special Cuts and Roasts.

Ground Beef:

Ground beef was my early-marriage-answer to meat for dinner. In the mid 1960's we had 2 babies, one paycheck and no credit cards. I could buy 3 or 4 pounds of ground beef for a dollar. We had all of the ground beef concoctions my mother had made and a few that I discovered on my own. Some of them, like stuffed cabbage rolls, stuffed peppers, tacos and nachos were pretty good. Other gems like porcupine meatballs and hamburger stroganoff were pathetic. I am only including one hamburger recipe.

Hunting Camp Meat Balls

This recipe is from a 1958, game cookbook I found at a flea market. The book claims 'there aren't any better meatballs and they are easy to make'.

They are right on both claims. The original recipe called for ground elk (or venison), butter, pork sausage, mashed potatoes, light cream and onion. I have changed most of the ingredients. I prefer using ground elk, but most of the time I use lean ground beef. Most of the supporting ingredients have also been substituted.

> 1 pound ground elk or venison or buffalo – or
> lean ground beef
> 1 egg, lightly beaten or 1½ tablespoon egg substitute
> ½ tablespoon olive oil
> ½ cup bread crumbs or Panko
> ½ cup light sour cream
> 1 teaspoon salt
> ½ teaspoon black pepper
> ½ cup diced shallots

Mix the ground meat with the egg. Add the remaining ingredients and mix thoroughly. Form the mixture into balls that are about I inch in diameter. Brown the meatballs in a skillet or a Dutch oven. Cover and simmer 30 for minutes. This recipe will serve 4 to 6.

Steaks:

As an adult I have found that many of the food items that have 'steak' in their title, like pork steak, chicken fried steak, or beef-steak tomatoes are truly mislabeled. Today if I have steak, chances are pretty good it came from a cow.

My husband and I rarely order steak in a restaurant because we like our home versions better. There are several good cuts of steak. I prefer top sirloin because it is fairly lean and flavorful. My husband likes rib steaks with lots of marbling. You may prefer something completely different. Regardless of the cut, there are some things you can do, like dry aging, to enhance the flavor and tenderness. I have included my never fail steak recipe as well as a chart on dry aging beef.

Never Fail Steak

The secret to a great steak is good meat, really high heat, salt and pepper. I brown the steak on top the stove in a cast-iron skillet and finish the cooking in the oven. There are no actual ingredient amounts. These are the guidelines:

- Buy fairly lean steak that is about 1½ inches thick. I recommend tenderloin, New York or top-sirloin steaks.
- Use a heavy, well seasoned cast-iron skillet. Preheat the skillet over high heat for 3 minutes. Add a scant ½ teaspoon of olive oil for each steak. Caution: Do not crowd the steaks. If you do, they will steam and get tough.
- Rub each steak with olive oil. Season with salt and pepper.
- Place the steaks in the hot skillet.

- Sear the steaks *without moving them* for 3 minutes.
- Turn the steaks over, sear another 3 minutes. Remove the skillet from the stovetop and place it in a preheated 450° oven.

Important: Follow the oven cooking times to achieve a perfect result

- very rare: 2 to 4 minutes (center is red and soft)
- rare: 6 to 8 minutes (center is pink and juicy)
- medium: 8 to 10 minutes (center is light pink, meat is firm)

To test steak, make a small cut with a paring knife and look inside. Remember the meat will continue to cook after you remove it from the oven.

If the steaks are *prefect* when you pull them out of the oven, you need to keep them that way. To halt the cooking process, splash a little red wine, preferably from the bottle you plan to drink with dinner. Sauces aren't necessary, but can be easily made with the pan juices.   Simply add minced shallots and mushrooms with Worcestershire sauce, Madeira, Dijon or whipping cream.

Special Cuts of Beef

Central Texas Brisket
This recipe is from my brother, Texas Larry. Larry is famous for his brisket and his BS. He is an undisputed expert at both. I believe he makes the BEST brisket ever. This recipe has a dozen or so steps and it takes about 3 days to make. All the steps are easy and most of them are necessary.

Ingredients:

1 whole or half untrimmed beef brisket
2 to 3 tablespoons yellow mustard
1 tablespoon Worcestershire Sauce
½ teaspoon garlic powder
2 tablespoons BBQ, or chili sauce
1 tablespoon of chili powder
½ teaspoon of hot Tabasco sauce
8 ounces beer

To prepare the meat:

Sear brisket over hot fire or BBQ grill. Don't try to burn off all the fat. The searing is to seal the brisket and to give it color. Place seared brisket in center of biggest, strongest, heaviest foil you can find. Smear (cheap) yellow mustard over top and bottom of brisket. Mix all spices together and pat into the top and bottom of the brisket. Pull up the sides of the foil and pour beer over the brisket.

- Wrap the foil around brisket and seal tightly.
- Prepare a second piece of foil. Place brisket on the foil, seam-side down. Wrap and seal tightly.
- Prepare a third piece of foil. Place brisket seam side down on the foil. Wrap and seal brisket making sure the foil is snug and tight. (When the brisket is slow cooked, the foil serves as a pressure cooker.)
- Place wrapped brisket in the refrigerator and to marinate for 6 to 36 hours.

To roast the brisket:
Place the wrapped brisket in a large roasting or broiler pan. Bake about 2 ½ hours at 350°. Then, turn off oven, but don't remove the brisket until the oven has cooled off.
Do not open the foil.
Place the brisket (still in the roasting pan) in the refrigerator overnight.

To serve:
Pull away and discard the foil, but save all meat juices.
Trim the brisket, removing and discarding visible fat.
Slice into serving sized pieces, about ¼ inches thick.
Place sliced brisket back into juices heat through and serve.
The meat will be incredibly tender and flavorful.

Brisket notes: *The first time I made brisket on my own I screwed it up so bad I had to humble myself and ask my big brother for step-by-step instructions that anyone could follow. He grumbled a little and then complied. I followed this recipe and was a hero for at least a day.*

A whole brisket is BIG, about 18 pounds. I have made this recipe several times with half a brisket. When I started making brisket the cost per pound was just about a dollar a pound. The last time I checked it was $4.18 a pound. Larry has suggested smearing the brisket with mayonnaise instead of mustard but I haven't tried that yet.

Marinated Flank Steak
My husband and I took a Chinese Cooking Class at Clackamas High School in the early 1970's and learned several techniques. One recipe I still use is the basic marinade. I think it works best on Flank Steak. I make this often and I have never measured any of these

ingredients. This is the best approximation that I could come up with:

Indgredients:
½ cup soy sauce
1 tablespoon Worcestershire sauce
¼ cup vegetable oil
½ to ¾ cup booze (wine, or beer, or whiskey)
¼ cup honey or brown sugar
3 large cloves of fresh garlic, peeled and minced
6 to 8 nickel sized slices peeled fresh ginger
1 Whole flank steak 1 – 2 lbs

Prepare the marinade by combining all ingredients except the flank steak. Place a whole flank steak in a zip lock storage bag. Pour the marinade over the steak and seal the bag. Place in the refrigerator over-night or up to two days. Turn bag occasionally to evenly distribute the marinade.

To cook the steak:
Remove the steak from the bag. Discard the marinade. Grill steak over hot coals for 7 to 10 minutes per side. Allow meat to rest for about 5 minutes then slice thinly against the grain.

Graciously accept the compliments you are sure to receive.

Roasts:

Pot Roast Stew: An Elk Camp Favorite
For many years nothing stood in the way of the annual hunting trips. Each hunter was responsible for one meal. Ron's designated meal (my responsibility) was stew. Early on I started making the stew with elk or venison from the prior year's hunt. This was a great

idea, but there was a little problem. Hunting successes are sporadic and I have substituted beef for wild game on a numerous occasions. This recipe makes a lot, and the hunters polish it off in less than a day.

Meat:
3 pounds of meat. This can be venison, elk or beef - Use round bone pot roast, rump roast or boneless beef rib roast

Stock:
Use 3 cups (divided) of either water, chicken broth, or canned tomatoes. I use a combination of all three

Vegetables:
- 3 or more pounds of fresh root vegetables, i.e., potatoes, carrots, turnips, and parsnips. Cut vegetables into 1 inch pieces.
- 3 pounds of potatoes, peeled and cut into quarters
- 1 large sweet onion, peeled and coarsly chopped
- Flour, salt, pepper, herbs and spices – plus 2 bay leaves.
- ½ cup vegetable oil
- A small bunch of freshly chopped parsley, or 2 tablespoons of dried parsley

To make the stew:
Cut the meat into 1½ inch cubes. Dust the meat pieces with flour that has been seasoned with salt, pepper and fresh herbs. Heat 1½ tablespoons of vegetable oil in a heavy bottom skillet over medium high heat. Add cut up meat pieces, a few at a time and brown on all sides. Remove browned meat from skillet and place meat in a stock pot.

Add about 2 cups of liquids. This can be water, chicken stock, canned tomatoes or a combination of all three. Add parsley and bay leaves to the stock pot, cover the pot and simmer for 1 hour. Add the pared fresh vegetables to the stock pot, add more liquid if necessary.

Cover the stockpot and simmer over medium low heat for another hour.

Add peeled, cut up red or Yukon gold potatoes. Adjust seasonings. Add at least a cup red wine, beer or ale. Cook 45 minutes or until meat is very tender and the vegetables are done. This stew is very good when served the same day it was made, but it is even better a day or two later.

Note: There are several oven bags complete with seasonings. They're not as good, but they are easier.

Beef Tenderloin Filet

Beef tenderloin is very expensive, extremely tender, and almost impossible to ruin. It is however, less flavorful than some of the more muscular cuts. In this recipe the whole filet is stuffed with shallots and butter mushrooms, rubbed with mustard, salt and pepper, and roasted in a hot oven until it is medium rare. It is served with a sauce of fresh chanterelle mushrooms, butter and wine. It is very expensive and it is very good.

Ingredients:
3 tablespoons olive oil, divided
¼ pound shallots, minced
1 pound chanterelle mushrooms, finely chopped
1 filet, 3 to 5 pounds (1 pound should serve 3 to 4 people)
¼ cup Dijon mustard

½ cup fresh herbs: rosemary, sage, thyme, salt and pepper

Directions:

Heat 1 tablespoon of olive oil in a heavy sauté pan over medium high heat. Add the mushrooms and shallots to the pan and sauté until soft. Remove the pan and mushroom mixture from the heat source and set aside to cool.

Cut a pocket in meat lengthwise. Fill the fillet with the mushroom mixture and truss. Rub fillet first with the mustard then coat it with the fresh herbs, salt and pepper. Preheat the oven to 450°. Position the fillet in a rack. Place it in the oven.

Reduce the oven temperature to 350°. Roast for 30 minutes or more or until internal temperature is 130°, (Use an instant read meat thermometer). Remove roast from pan and allow it to rest for 10 minutes while you prepare the sauce.

Chanterelle Mushroom Sauce:

¼ cup butter
8 ozs. fresh chanterelle mushrooms, sliced
Roasting pan juices
1¾ cups Pinot Noir wine
½ cup beef stock
½ cup heavy cream

Melt ¼ cup butter in sauté pan over medium heat. Add 8 ounces sliced chanterelles and sauté gently until the mushrooms are soft. Deglaze the pan used to roast tenderloin over medium high heat. Pour ½ cup water into the pan, add ½ cup wine. Scrape the pan bottom to loosen any bits of meat that are left from the roast. Add the chanterelles mixture, heat and stir to blend together. Finish the sauce by adding the beef broth and heavy cream to mushroom mixture.

To Serve:
Slice meat into serving-sized pieces and ladle the sauce over the meat.

Beef Stock Note: If you don't have home-made beef stock, use canned, **low sodium** stock.

Chanterelle note: *I had this recipe for several years before I scored some fresh Chanterelles Mushrooms and gave it a try. In the fall, after the first heavy rain, wild Chanterelle mushrooms start appearing in the Douglas Fir forests on the west side of the coastal range. We found a "Chanterelle Stand" that sells fresh beauties for $3 to $6 a pound. The stand is near Banks, Oregon on the way to the coast.*

In fall, 2003, I prepared this dish with the chanterelles and it was fabulous. I loved it, but I got really sick after eating it. I tried eating chanterelles three more times, and each time I got sick. Apparently I have acquired an allergy to chanterelles. It's just not fair. I still love chanterelles, but I will never eat them again. Damn.

Becky's Roast Beef
This is my recipe. It makes the best beef roast that I have ever tasted. Again, my own recipes are created with on-hand ingredients and uncharted imagination. All ingredient amounts are estimates.
- Buy a large roast, at least 3 pounds I recommend a beef sirloin roast
- Marinate the roast overnight with the following:
- Equal parts soy sauce and red wine
- Fresh garlic, minced
- Fresh ginger, thinly sliced
- Fresh ground pepper

- 2 to 3 tablespoons vegetable oil

Prepare the marinade making sure that all ingredients have been incorporated. Place roast in a large self-sealing plastic zip lock bag, and pour the marinade over the roast. Allow the meat to marinate for at least 4 hours or as long as 2 days. Remove the meat from the marinade. Dry meat off and discard any leftover marinade. Rub the roast with a purchased pepper rub.

Preheat oven to 450° and place meat on rack. Roast 50 minutes to 1 hour until internal temperature is 130° (use an instant read meat thermometer).

Note: My roast beef recipe is still very good and very reliable, but it has been bumped out of first place by a Cook's Magazine recipe that I call Christmas Roast Beef.

Cooks Christmas Roast Beef

Cook's Illustrated© is a cooking magazine. Their target audience is people who appreciate really good food and would like to replicate that food at home. It is a *'how to with specific products and ingredients to use'* type of magazine. I subscribe to this magazine and several recipes from Cook's are included in this family cookbook. One issue of Cook's Magazine focused on the 'best' beef roasts and steaks.

The best holiday roast beef is a multi-step process that relies on the best cut of meat and dry aging it 1 to 3 days before it is roasted.

The magazine compared several different cuts of meat. They selected a boneless New York Steak roast with the following rational:

- Standing Rib Roast; "Bones give roast great flavor, but they are a hassle when it comes to carving."

- Beef Tenderloin: " A tenderloin is easy to cook and carve, but the flavor is thin."
- Top Sirloin Roast: "This roast has minimal marbling, and several muscles that are separated by connective tissue. The result is a roast that is too chewy."
- The winning roast was boneless Top Loin, also known as New York Strip Roast because, "This roast contains a single muscle and a good amount of marbling it also has more flavor."

I decided to try it for our Christmas dinner. I ordered a six pound *boneless* New York roast, but when I picked it up I got a 6 pound roast with bone. I had to improvise. First, I set the roast on a rack inside the refrigerator for 3 days.

When it was time to cook the roast I trimmed most of the outside fat and allowed it to set for 1 hour at room temperature. I rubbed the roast with a little olive oil, salt and a prepared pepper rub. The roast was seared on top the oven over high heat before roasting. I used a cast-iron skillet. After browning the roast I turned it fat side down and placed it in the same cast iron skillet into a preheated 350° oven. I checked it frequently and removed the roast when the internal temperature was 120 to 125°. The roast was allowed to rest for 20 minutes before it was boned and sliced into ¼ inch slices. It was easy. And it was the BEST roast EVER. My family loved this roast and their dogs truly enjoyed the bones.

The following information regarding dry aging is taken directly from Cook's Magazine.

SCIENCE: **A Ripe Old Age**

Every butcher knows that aging meat in a very cold refrigerator makes it more tender and flavorful. Even the English in the Middle Ages (not a group of folks who were known for their haute cuisine) hung their meat for a long time to improve its flavor until it literally dropped from the hook. But how does aging work?

Two processes occur in dry aging. In one, called proteolysis, an enzyme turns stiff muscle fibers into tender meat. The other process is simply dehydration. In dry aging, a roast can lose up to 25 percent of its original weight. Less water means more concentrated flavors.

Although a few high-end butchers and restaurants dry-age their meat, today most meat is "wet-aged"—vacuum-sealed in plastic. Wet-aged beef is tender, but it does not lose any moisture (or weight) as it ages, making wet aging a much more economical process than dry aging. However, wet-aged beef is not as flavorful as dry-aged beef, something we've noticed in repeated tastings in the test kitchen over the years. (Dry-aged beef has nutty, buttery notes that just aren't present in wet-aged beef.) By letting a wet-aged roast from the supermarket age in the refrigerator for just a short period, we found we could approximate the dehydrating effects of dry aging at home, with an eye to improving the flavor rather than the texture of the meat. —John Olson

I have since tired dry-aging on a New York boneless steak. The steak was placed on a shallow dish and kept uncovered in the refrigerator for 2 days. When I cooked it, the meat was tender, juicy and very flavorful. I repeated this experiment with other varieties of beef roasts.

Add your favorite beef notes and recipes here…

2. REAL MEAT; Pork

In Waukegan, we ate pork marbled with fat. It was tender and flavorful. For breakfast, we had bacon, or pork sausage. Mom saved bacon-grease and used it for fried potatoes and other things.

She made pork chops about once a month. Our pork chops were thin, bony, and layered in fat. Mom cooked them in a little bacon grease over high heat until they were brown outside and colorless inside. For years this was her signature dish.

Grandma Mabel's Famous Pork Chops and Rice
    1 center-cut pork chop per person
    3 Cups cooked white rice (mom used Uncle Ben's)
    1 can Campbell's cream of Chicken Soup
Directions:
Prepare rice according to package instructions. Pan-fry pork chops in skillet until lightly browned. Butter an ovenproof casserole dish. Press cooked rice into dish and top with pork chops. Heat soup in the same skillet used to brown pork chops. Add a little milk to soup mixture. Pour soup mixture over pork chops. Bake 30 minutes in 350° oven

Pork included bacon, sausage, pork steaks, pork chops and ham.
We all liked ham; Dad loved it. He especially liked the slabs of white ham-fat that was just under the skin. About once a month Mom bought a large bone-in ham.

Ham was like a play that is destined to run for a while:

- Act 1 was baked ham dinner, but that was only the beginning.
- Act II was ham sandwiches.
- Act III was fried ham pieces for breakfast.
- Act IV was the best, ham and scalloped potatoes.

The final act was called 'boiled dinner.' The ham bone was covered with water and boiled with cabbage, onions, carrots and potatoes. At my house a large ham never lasted more than five days.

I don't ever remember eating pork roast or pork cutlets. If Mom had roasted a fresh ham or a pork shoulder, it would have been roasted, uncovered, for a long time in a 350° oven. The high percentage of fat would have kept the meat juicy. In those days, lean pork was unthinkable.

Pigs were more apt to grow wings and fly then to ever become lean! That was true up until the early 1990's when farmers began raising leaner hogs.

Today pork is known as the other white meat and it provides a tasty alternative to chicken. Pork fat still has a home in sausage and bacon, but lean pork is now the rule rather than the exception.
Most of the pork recipes I prepare call for roasts cut from the 'loin section. This section includes: loin roast, with or without rib bones. A crown roast created by a butcher who bends two loin sections to form a crown with its rib bones, sirloin, near the rump, and the tenderloin. Pork is generally roasted, uncovered at 350°. Moisture needs to be added to keep juices and flavor in. See chart on page 38 for details.

Pork Tenderloins

This versatile cut of meat lies next to the backbone. It is lean, tender and flavorful. Pork tenderloins weigh anywhere between 10 to 12 ounces up to 2 pounds. There are dozens of recipes featuring pork tenderloin. Unlike other pork roasts, the tenderloin can be roasted in a very hot oven or even cooked atop the stove. The USDA recommends cooking pork to an internal temperature of 165°. The maximum temperature for lean pork is 160°. In order to achieve that temperature, the pork roast should be removed from the oven when it registers 155° on an instant read thermometer.

Pork Tenderloin with Maple Glaze: Serves 6
*This recipe is based on a recipe I found in Bon Appetite. I was intrigued by this recipe because it is cooked on top of the stove rather than in the oven. I have changed several of the ingredients, but the maple syrup had to stay. The key may be using **real** maple syrup. I have tried this recipe with thick boneless pork chops and it is great.*

> 12 to 14 ounce pork tenderloin
> 2 tablespoons minced fresh herbs, thyme, basil
> and/or tarragon or 2 teaspoons dried herbs
> ½ tablespoon butter
> ½ tablespoon olive oil
> 4 tablespoons pure maple syrup
> 3 tablespoons apple cider vinegar or rice wine vinegar, divided
> ¾ teaspoon Dijon mustard

Directions:
Rub tenderloins with fresh or dried herbs, then season with salt and pepper. Heat the butter and olive oil in a large, heavy non-stick (or cast-iron) skillet over medium high heat. Add the tenderloin to the skillet and brown on all sides. This will take about 6 minutes. Reduce the heat to medium low. Cover and continue to cook about

10 minutes or until pork registers 155°. Transfer pork to platter. Cover to keep warm.

Glaze:

Whisk the maple syrup, 1 tablespoon of vinegar and Dijon mustard together in a small bowl. Set aside. Return the skillet to the stove top and increase the heat to medium high. Add the 2 remaining tablespoons of vinegar and bring to a boil. Stir, scraping up any browned bits from the bottom of the skillet. Reduce the heat and return the pork to skillet with any meat juices. Add the maple syrup mixture and coat the tenderloin with the glaze. This will take about 2 minutes. Remove from the heat. Cut the pork tenderloin into ½ inch slices and season with salt and pepper.

To serve: Arrange pork slices on plates. Spoon glaze over pork and serve.

When I use this recipe for large boneless pork chops, the primary ingredients don't change but the timing and cooking methods are different. The chops that I use are about 2 inches thick and weigh at least 8 ounces apiece. They do not cook nearly as fast as the tenderloin.

This is my method:

I always us a cast iron skillet and I always use equal amounts of butter and olive oil when I sear any meat. The chops are first browned quickly on all sides over medium high heat. The heat is reduced to low, and a cup of liquid is added. The liquid can be water or a mixture of water and apple cider. Sprinkle the chops with fresh or dried herbs and arrange equal portions of sliced sweet onions or shallots and peeled tart apple slices around the chops. Cover the skillet and simmer for up 1 hour. Check the skillet every 15 minutes, turn the chops and add additional liquids as necessary. The maple syrup mixture shown above is added to the pan drippings when the chops are very tender. Thin the mixture with a little water or light sour cream. Add salt and pepper to taste and serve with the sauce ladled over the chops or on the side.

Char Siu Pork, Chinese Barbecue Pork
You can purchase Char Siu Pork at any Chinese restaurant and in many deli's. Char Siu is the tender, thinly sliced pork that is usually served with hot mustard as an appetizer. It is recognized by the bright red coloring on the outside. I make this dish at home using a prepared mix made by NOH® of Hawaii. I simply rub it on the raw pork and let it set in the refrigerator for a couple hours. The tenderloin is roasted in a hot, 400° oven for about 20 minutes.
Note: Most large grocery stores have this type of mix.

Pork Loins, Center Loin and Blade Cuts

The blade end loin is closer to the shoulder and has more fat than the sirloin or the tenderloin. It can range in size from 5 to 7 pounds. There are scores of pork loin recipes. Most are roasted in the oven. The loin is too lean to be dry roasted. New recipes feature brining, marinating and/or glazing the pork to seal in juices and enhance flavor.

Roasted Stuffed Pork Loin
This is a modified recipe from Cook's Magazine. They developed it for a special or Holiday meal. Cook's had two concerns: The stuffing would not be cooked long and hot enough to kill any/all bacteria associated with eggs or ground meat. If the stuffing was cooked long enough, the meat would be dry and overcooked. Their solution was to brine, butterfly and pound out the roast for even cooking; braise it for flavor and color and to stuff it with pre-cooked stuffing. I wanted to try this recipe for several reasons:

- I hadn't given much thought to undercooked stuffing and the related health concerns. (When my children read that last statement I guarantee their comment will be: "No kidding.")
- I had brined a turkey with terrific results. I was interested to see what brining could do to pork. The recipe is simple, but it takes some pre-planning.

Ingredients:

4½ pound pork loin roast: Choose a roast that is cut from the blade end loin, the wider part of the loin, so it will be uniform in thickness.

¾ cup sugar

¾ cup kosher salt or 6 tablespoons of table salt

3 bay leaves, crumbled

1 tablespoon whole all spice berries, crushed

1 tablespoon black peppercorns, crushed

10 cloves garlic, peeled and crushed

Stuffing: Prepare a dressing or stuffing of your choice.
Glaze: ½ cup apricot preserves

Trim off the tough silver skin from the pork loin. Butterfly the loin and pound to 1 inch thickness. Combine sugar and salt with 3 cups of hot water. Add spices and 5 cups of cold water. Stir until sugar and salt have dissolved then add prepared pork loin. Cover and refrigerate for 90 minutes. Use your favorite recipe for dressing. Form dressing into a log about the same length as the pork roast. Cover stuffing with foil and bake 45 minutes at 325° while the pork is brining.

Remove the pork roast from the brine. Rinse with cold water. Press the sides of the roast together. Secure the roast at regular intervals with sharp bamboo skewers. With the skewers in place, tie the roast together with kitchen twine. Cut off the ends of the skewers. Place the roast on a V shaped rack and brush ½ the roast with ½ the glaze. Roast for 20 minutes. Remove the roast from the oven and rotate it and brush with the remaining glaze. Roast for 25 minutes longer. Use a meat thermometer to check for doneness. The internal temperature should be 155°. Remove from oven and allow to rest for 10 minutes. Remove the twine, slice and serve.

Pork Loin, Brined and Roasted – My Version

Note: I made the recipe shown above absolutely according to the directions only once. It was very good, but it took more time, energy and pre-planning than I could muster a second time around. I have adapted this recipe to my life style.

- I do not butterfly, pound out, or stuff
- I use the apricot glaze, but it is diluted with 1 little water, a tablespoon of soy sauce and a ½ tablespoon of olive oil.
- It is roasted at 350° for 2½ to 3 hours or until the internal temperature is 150°. It needs to rest at least 20 minutes.
- While the loin is resting, the pan juices are combined with a little water, some sautéed shallots and mushrooms. This makes a rich, dark sauce that is softened a little by the addition of ¼ cup of heavy or light sour cream.
- The meat is sliced and served with the sauce ladled over the top or on the side.

Pork Cutlets

The first time I encountered pork cutlets was on a breakfast menu. They were called chicken fried steak and served with fried eggs and homemade biscuits under a blanket of milk-based sausage gravy. My husband had eaten this concoction before and he jumped at the chance to have it again. I tasted it, although it appeared to be a contradiction in terms, it tasted good. I don't make this at home and I have never ordered it at a restaurant.

Shredded Pork

- Buy a pork shoulder or a boneless pork loin. Season it with salt and pepper the put it in a crock pot for about 8 hours. It will fall apart when you touch it and I swear to God it will be tender and can be easily pulled apart. Shredded pork aka pulled pork is versatile:
- Add prepared commercial Bar-B-Que Sauce for a great sandwich.
- Use as a filling for tacos and/or enchiladas.

RIBS!

Pork ribs are bony, fatty, hard to eat, and expensive. In my opinion, the *only* reason anyone would eat these things is because they taste so darn GOOD.I have given up trying to make ribs. When we need a rib fix, we go to Tony Romas or to Buster's Barbeque. There are also pre-cooked packages of baby-back ribs available in most grocery stores.

Pork Chops!

Most butcher blocks sell boneless pork chops that are cut about 2 inches thick. My method of cooking these mini-roasts is a little unconventional, but the results are tasty, tender and pretty darn easy. They are quickly browned in olive oil, then are seared on the stove-top, and cooked in the oven at 350° for about 30 minutes.

Roasting Pork, General Guidelines:

Roast pork at 350°. Roast on a rack in a shallow pan, uncovered. Take roast out of the oven when the internal temperature reaches 155°. Final temperature should be 160°.

Cut	Location and Description	Weight	Minutes per pound
Loin Roast – blade end	Close to the shoulder – higher fat content	2 - 5 pounds	20 - 30
Sirloin Roast or chops	Close to the rump – low in fat but can contain part of hip and backbone	4 - 6 pounds	20 to 30
Center Loin Roast	Between shoulder and rump	3 - 6 pounds	20 to 30
Fresh ham, whole bone-in	Leg	12 -16 pounds	22 to 26
Fresh ham, half, bone-in	Leg	5 – 8 pounds	35 to 40
Boston butt	Shoulder – low cost/high fat	3 – 6 pounds	45
Tenderloin Roast at 425° - 450°	Next to the spine	½ - 2 pounds	20 to 30 minutes total time

Add your favorite pork recipes here.

Beyond the City Limits

3. FOWL MEAT: CHICKEN

On Sunday, every Sunday after church we would have fried chicken dinner. Everyone in Waukegan, throughout Illinois, the entire Midwest, and probably the WORLD had fried chicken every Sunday. Every wife and mother worth her salt could fry a good chicken, or she would never hear the end of it. It was some kind of culinary law.

Mom made pretty good fried chicken. She would cut up the chicken, dredge it in salted flour, and fry the pieces until golden brown in hot melted Crisco ©. The idea was to have the skin crispy, and the chicken done. Mom served fried chicken with mashed potatoes, a milk-flour gravy, peas and baking powder biscuits. This was "Sunday's Best Cooking." When I was growing up it was my absolute favorite meal. Every wife and mother worth her salt could fry a good chicken, or she never heard the end of it.

Sometime during the 1950's a bearded old codger, Colonel Sanders, came out with his <u>secret</u> recipe for Kentucky Fried Chicken®. The TV ads said it was 'finger licking' good!'
Well, it was pretty good. Almost everyone, including the husbands, liked it and KFC caught on. The wives considered the Colonel's chicken a threat to their status, reputation, and to supremacy in the kitchen. They started fighting back and the battle was on: Which housewife could make fried chicken that tasted as good as the Colonel's?
The wives started trying to improve a good thing. First, they had to crack the secret code and

 *There were 11 Secret Herbs and Spices!*

- They tried adding pepper, and paprika, MSG and other exotic spices in addition to salt.

- They tried cornmeal and pancake mix with or instead of flour.
- They tried breading with bread crumbs, then with crushed corn flakes.
- They tried adding bacon grease and/or oleo to the Crisco®
- Some women even tried smearing the chicken with mayonnaise
-

(My mom didn't do that. Of course she would have had to use Miracle Whip® because there was no mayonnaise at the Edwards's house on Butrick Street. Ever.)

The Chicken Wars, as they came to be known were serious. We started having chicken more than once a week and my dad was in pig heaven. He loved it. He would lick his fingers and say," Mabel, you're getting closer. Keep trying!"

Mom made good fried chicken but she couldn't hold a candle to Aunt Hattie.

Grandpa Aldridge had a half sister, Harriett Gunderson. Aunt Hattie lived on a small farm near the Eau Claire River in north central Wisconsin. We would stop at her place and spend the night whenever we made a trip to Northern Michigan. Aunt Hattie was old, but very capable. I thought she had a wonderful place. The river was across the road, and we could go swimming. There was a family cemetery on her property. My sister Sharon and I liked to explore the cemetery and try to find the connection between those old grave-stones and our family.

Best of all, Aunt Hattie raised pigs and chickens! We pitched corn cobs at the pigs. (I don't know why that was so much fun.) And then there were the chickens. 'Running around like a chicken with its

head cut off' was a fairly common phrase in the 1950's. I had heard that phrase, but I didn't understand what it meant until I watched Aunt Hattie whack a chicken. It truly did run around headless. Bright red blood squirted up and out. The circles became smaller and smaller until the headless chicken fell over. Aunt Hattie scalded that chicken, dressed it and cooked it.
Colonel Sanders had nothing on my Aunt Hattie. It was the best fried chicken in the world.

Aunt Hattie is gone. So are true farm-fresh chickens.

Today, chickens cover the following categories:

1. **Hens that lay eggs: I believe that when their egg production falls off, (spent hens) they are marketed as roasters or sold to FDA lunch programs. .**
2. **Roosters: These birds are also known as 'cocks.' They strut, cluck and service the hens.**
3. **Eggs: This prolific chicken product is snatched from the hens and sold.**
4. **Fryers: These are young, male chickens that are raised commercially for a few weeks and then slaughtered. They are marketed as fryers. They are tender, flavorful and very fatty.**

My sister found one of mom's cookbooks from the early 1970's, after our folks had moved to Tucson. Mom appears to be branching out a little and trying some pre-packaged ingredients. Her book had 2 recipes for chicken:

The first recipe is oven barbequed chicken, it calls for a whole chicken. The second recipe features left over chicken or turkey.

Oven Barbequed Chicken with Crispy Biscuits

2½ to 3 pound whole chicken
1 cup prepared barbequed sauce
10 ounce can of Hungry Jack Biscuits®
½ cup shredded cheese

Directions:
Heat oven to 400°
Grease a 13 x 9 inch pan
Dip whole chicken in barbeque sauce. Place in prepared pan skin side up.
Bake for 40 to 45 minutes or until tender.
Move chicken to one side of the pan.
Separate biscuit dough into 10 biscuits. Sprinkle with cheese.
Bake 15 to 20 minutes or until biscuits are golden brown.

Chick-N- Broccoli Pot Pies

10 ounce can Hungry Jack Biscuits®
2/3 cup shredded American or cheddar cheese
2/3 cup crispy rice cereal
2 tablespoons margarine
1 cup cubed chicken or turkey
1- 10 ounce can of cream of mushroom soup
10 ounce package of frozen broccoli, cooked and drained
½ cup silvered almonds

Directions:
Heat oven to 375°
Separate biscuit dough into 10 biscuits. Place each biscuit into a muffin pan.
Press dough to cover bottom and sides

Add a little cheese, then cereal and a dab of margarine to each cup Combine chicken, soup and broccoli. Spoon about 1/3 cup over cereal mixture in each cup. Sprinkle slivered almonds over the top. Bake casserole at 375° for 20 to 25 minutes or until biscuits are golden brown.

Serve with cheese sauce or slivered almonds if desired.

Disclaimer: *I don't fry chicken, and I have never tried either of Mom's 'new' chicken recipes. However, I buy and cook a lot of chicken. My husband says if he has chicken one more day a week he will start to cluck! I have divided the recipes into those calling for chicken breasts and those using either a whole chicken or different parts of the chicken.*

Roast Chicken Breasts with Parsley Pan Gravy
This is really easy and pretty good. The main reason I included it was because it features a very hot oven. I think that's the way chicken (that hasn't been skinned and boned) should be cooked. Bake at 475° for 25 Minutes.

1 chicken breast with skin and bones, halved
1 teaspoon poultry seasoning
Salt and pepper
1 tablespoon butter, cut into small pieces
1 tablespoon flour
1/3 cup chicken broth
¼ cup chopped parsley

To prepare the chicken:
Use your fingers to loosen skin on chicken breast and rub half the poultry season on each half breast under the skin. Season each breast with salt and pepper. Place chicken breasts skin side up in a cast iron or other oven proof skillet, and dot with butter. Roast chicken at

475° until the breasts are tender, about 25 minutes. Remove breasts from the oven and transfer chicken to serving plate. Place pan with juices over burner on medium high heat. Add flour to the pan juices and stir until brown. Whisk in the chicken broth and bring to boil until mixture thickens, 2 minutes. Add parsley and season with salt and pepper. This dish serves 2.

Chicken Curry
This is easy and good. It is a wonderful rebirth for leftover chicken or turkey.
Important hints:
1. *Buy good curry*
2. *Use Gravenstein apples*

Ingredients:
1 tablespoon olive oil
¼ cup sweet onion, chopped
2 cups tart apple, peeled, cored and chopped
2 tablespoons flour
½ teaspoon salt
¼ teaspoon ginger
1 teaspoon curry powder
1 cup skimmed milk
1½ cups cooked chicken, diced
¼ cup dried cranberries
2 cups cooked rice (prepared per package instructions)

Directions:
Slowly cook onion and apple in olive oil until tender. Stir in the flour, salt, ginger and curry powder.
Add milk slowly and stir until thickened. Add chicken and cranberries. Heat through.
Serve over rice.

Chicken Newhouse

This is a quick, easy summer recipe. It is great for a dinner and it can be doubled or tripled for parties. This version serves 8. I'd guess this recipe was inspired by someone who spent some time in Greece.

Ingredients:
3 to 4 pounds boneless, skinless chicken breasts
¼ cup olive oil
¼ cup dried basil, (see note)
½ pound feta cheese crumbled into evenly sized chunks
2 cups diced celery and/or red pepper cut into ½ inch strips or a sliced onion and red pepper

Directions:
Cut chicken breasts into thin 1 inch strips. Heat oil in large non-stick pan or wok. Add chicken and vegetables to the pan and cook until done. Reduce heat. Add basil and feta cheese. Cook until feta begins to melt. Serve over cooked pasta or rice.
Note: *Fresh basil makes this dish even better.*

The following chicken recipes feature something other than chicken breasts.
Some require a whole chicken, others call for chicken thighs. I have cooked all these recipes, and they are reliably good. Some of the recipes I truly have followed to the letter. However, many of them are changed or modified with each cooking. Perhaps it is time I explained my overall cooking philosophy.

I believe that real food recipes are always a suggestion, not a formula. It is acceptable to substitute one cut of meat or spice or flavor for another without any real harm. The result of such creativity (or carelessness) is simply a dish that is a little different.

On rare, very rare occasions, the changes don't work and the result is a complete disaster. When that happens we go out to eat!

Based on my philosophy, some of the following recipes have only suggestions in lieu of actual ingredients or amounts. That's the great thing about cooking real food versus desserts. Dessert recipes are formulas and they have to be followed. Thank goodness we are still in the realm of real food.

Whole Chickens Baked on a Vertical Roaster

Vertical roasters are sold at kitchen and specialty stores and used to cook a whole chicken. The chicken is cleaned, seasoned with salt and pepper and baked for about an hour at 425°. As the chicken cooks, the fat simply drains from the chicken into the base of the roaster. The skin gets very crisp, and the chicken is moist and flavorful. Sometimes I loosen the skin around the breast and stuff with fresh herbs and feta or blue cheese. I am always amazed at the amount of fat that comes off a fryer.

I buy 4 or 5 whole chickens whenever they are on sale. (If Ron is with me at the time of purchase he loses most of his color and starts clucking.)
Even I know 4 or 5 is an obscene amount of chicken, but never fear, I have a plan:

I bake one on the vertical roaster but that is only the beginning. In truth, I cut the remaining chickens up and turn them every way but loose. The breasts are cut in two, skinned, boned and repackaged into ½ chicken-breast bundles for future meals.

The various parts, legs, thighs and wings are packed in sandwich bags and then stored in larger freezer bags. When you buy a whole chicken you are stuck with the fat, chicken neck, back, liver, heart, gizzard and all the skin and bones.

I boil all the scraps for home-made chicken stock, but that still leaves the internal organs. I used to either throw these things in the garbage, or occasionally I would cook them and feed them to the dog.

And then the dog died, (not from my cooking) and I discovered that my husband loved chicken livers. I still throw away the heart and gizzard, but now I keep the livers. The following chicken-liver recipe is full of suggestions and void of any specific amounts.

Chicken Livers
I made these for Ron's mother and received an A+. I never eat them. You will need some, (certainly more than 1) chicken liver. The liver from a small fryer really isn't worth the time and trouble it takes to fix it. Either buy a bunch of fryers on sale, cut them up and save livers from 3 or 4 fryers or splurge and buy a pound of livers.

- Rinse the livers, cut up into manageable pieces. Dredge with seasoned flour. Shake off excess flour and set aside.
- Slice 4 or 5 large mushrooms. Sauté them in equal parts of butter and olive oil over medium high heat until the mushroom slices lose their moisture and are nicely browned. This takes 5 to 8 minutes.
- Add finely chopped shallots to skillet. Sauté for a minute or two, then add the chicken livers. When the chicken livers are lightly browned, reduce heat and add a little water, wine, or brandy. Cover the sauté pan and simmer for 10 minutes or until chicken livers are done.

Middle East Grilled Herbed Chicken

Ingredients:
½ cup finely chopped Italian parsley
½ cup finely chopped fennel tops *or* 2 teaspoons
dried fennel seeds
½ cup finely chopped green onions
8oz. carton plain non-fat yogurt
-Salt and pepper
1- 3 pound whole chicken butterflied
1 teaspoon olive oil

Butterfly the chicken then clean it and remove the excess fat. Combine the first 5 ingredients in a small bowl then place the mixture under the chicken's skin. Massage the chicken to evenly distribute the seasonings. Let chicken stand at least 30 minutes or refrigerate uncovered overnight.

To Cook: Brush with olive oil. Grill, skin side up 45 to 55 minutes or bake in conventional oven at 425° for about 1 hour.

I have not shared the wonders of Hawaiian Chicken, which is kind of like this but deep fried with green peppers and pineapple. It is Nasty. There were some other swell cheap creations I used to make. They're long gone.

Scandinavian Chicken

This dish is easy, and most people like it. I rarely cook it because it reminds me of the casserole dishes I made when we first got married. This one is better than most.

Ingredients:
6 chicken thighs, skinned, boned

and cut into 1" pieces
1½ tablespoons butter
1½ tablespoons olive oil
1 teaspoon salt
¼ teaspoon pepper
2/3 cup finely chopped onion
8 oz fresh mushrooms, sliced
¾ cup sour cream
½ cup shredded Havarti cheese
  – *exactly how does one shred havarti cheese?*
¼ cup fresh bread crumbs or Panko
1 to 2 tablespoons of fresh parsley

Use a heavy bottomed large sauté pan or a cast iron skillet. Place the pan over medium high heat. Add the butter and olive oil to the pan, heat until butter melts and then add the chicken pieces. Cook the chicken until it is browned. This takes about 7 minutes. Add the chopped onion and cook another 5 minutes. Add the mushrooms and cook 5 minutes more. Reduce the heat and stir in the sour cream and cheese and cook until the cheese melts. Season with salt and pepper, and sprinkle with parsley and breadcrumbs. Serve with rice or noodles.

Roast Chicken with Morels

This is simply a baked whole fryer, but it is stuffed with wonderful mushrooms and served with a fantastic cream sauce. My husband, who is sick to death of chicken, thinks this is pretty close to damn good. I think part of the secret is baking the chicken in a really hot oven. The skin is crispy. The meat is done. The sauce is worth the calories.

Ingredients:
2 ozs dried morels, chanterelles or porcini mushrooms
3 tablespoons butter, divided
½ cup whipping cream
♦ Salt and freshly ground pepper
1 whole chicken, 3½ pounds
¼ cup white wine
1 cup chicken broth
¾ cup cream fraiche
1 teaspoon fresh lemon juice

Directions:
Place cut up dried mushrooms in a bowl with hot water. Soak for one hour. Melt 1 tablespoon of butter in a sauté pan and add the mushrooms. Sauté for 5 minutes then add the cream. Continue to cook until sauce is reduced by ½ then season with salt and pepper and remove from the heat.

Rub chicken inside and out with butter. Spoon the mushroom mixture into the cavity. Place chicken breast side up in an oven proof baking dish that can also be used on top of the stove. I use a cast-iron skillet.

Roast chicken breast side up for 45 min at 450°. Turn chicken breast side down and roast another 15 minutes. Finally, turn chicken breast side up, roast 5 more minutes and then remove it from the oven.

Transfer the chicken to a carving board. Pour most of fat from the skillet and discard. Place the skillet over medium high heat. Add wine and cook until juices are reduced to a glaze. Add chicken broth and continue to cook until reduced by half. Add the mushroom mixture from the cavity and cream fraiche. Continue to reduce the sauce. Add the chicken juices from the platter and cook until smooth and add salt and pepper to taste.

Cut chicken into serving pieces, boning the breast section. Serve with mushroom sauce over the chicken and along side.

Shanghai Chicken Cakes with Saucy Plum Sauce
This recipe came from Food Day. I have made it several times. It is a bit of a project and it makes 8 to 10 chicken cakes so we usually cook up 3 or 4 and freeze the rest individually. I really love good crab cakes. I think these chicken cakes are as good as or better than the best crab cakes.

This is my wordy way of saying that they are worth the trouble.

Chicken Cakes:
3 cups cooked chicken, finely chopped

2 cloves garlic, minced
1/3 cup minced green onion
1 tablespoon minced ginger root
1 cup Panko (Japanese bread crumbs) divided

¼ cup Mascarpone cheese
1 well beaten egg
1 tablespoon soy sauce
¼ cup sweet-hot chili sauce
¼ cup sesame seeds
2 tablespoons dark sesame oil

Saucy Plum Sauce

¾ cup bottled Chinese plum sauce
¼ cup hot chili sauce
1 tablespoon soy sauce
¼ cup minced green onion

1 tablespoon toasted sesame seeds

Directions: To Make Chicken Cakes
- Mix chicken with garlic, onion, ginger, half the Panko crumbs, cheese, egg, soy sauce and chili sauce. Shape mixture into 8 pancakes (about 3 ½ inch diameter)

- Mix sesame seeds with remaining ½ cup Panko crumbs. Coat cakes on both sides of the pancakes with the Panko mixture.
- Heat the sesame oil in large heavy skillet. Add the pancakes. Cook about 3 minutes per side or until nicely browned. Serve with Saucy plum sauce.

Directions: Saucy Plum Sauce

Mix plum sauce, chili sauce and soy sauce together. Put into a serving bowl. Sprinkle with onion and sesame seeds. Add dark sesame oil.

Add your favorite chicken recipes here.

4. FOWL MEAT: TURKEY

We had turkey <u>once</u> a year, for Thanksgiving dinner. Thanksgiving was a family holiday, a time to get together with adult brothers and sisters. Mom always wanted to spend every holiday with her folks and her brothers. That was okay for the 4th of July, but the winter holidays were a different matter. Mom would get blue and start moping around the house in early November. She would ask dad if we could be with her folks for the holiday.

My dad would convince her, in his own kind way, that a trip to the Copper Country, 400 miles away, for a meal and a long weekend simply was not possible. I can almost hear him:

"Mabel! Don't be ridiculous! It's already winter up there. They have 6 feet of snow on the ground and a blizzard on the way."
Then he would shake his head.
"Jesus Mabel, what were you thinking?"

Dad would continue to mutter and sputter as he walked away. It was his contention that in northern Michigan, the Copper Country, they had 11 months of winter and 1 month of bad weather.

Dad's brothers and father lived in town. His sister Margaret was in nearby in Racine, Wisconsin. Aunt Harriet was further away, in Madison, Wisconsin. We saw her less often. Usually, we had Thanksgiving at my Uncle Sherman's house. They had a big eating area with enough room for all the adults at the main table and overflow tables here and there for the kids.

I never made it to the adult table. By the time I was old enough, I was gone. Aunt Shirley made the turkey, Mom would bring the pies and the rest of the family would fill in with the potatoes, sweet and white, peas, and cranberries. It was a feast, and we would eat until we couldn't walk. I really don't remember how good the turkey was. I ate pie and played with my cousins.

I also remember one Thanksgiving dinner at 'Aunt' Edythe's. Edythe wasn't really an aunt. She was a nurse and my mom's best friend. She was always a little ahead of her time. One year she made turkey stuffing with oysters. I like oysters, now. At that time I would not even consider trying it.

By the time I was ready for college, my brother, Larry already owned a restaurant. He was an accomplished cook and willing to try anything new. One year he cooked a turkey in the Weber charcoal grill. It was good. After Larry's success, Mom tried turkey cooked in a brown paper bag, in a plastic oven cooking bag, and in a roaster. They were all good.

Larry's last turkey discovery was deep fried. He convinced my husband to buy a turkey fryer. I prepared the turkey according to Larry's instructions and Ron cooked it.

Ron loved deep fried turkey. It is pretty good, and strange as it might seem, it's not greasy, but I swear I heard some of my arteries slam shut when I ate this meal. Larry thinks it is great, so do Ron's hunting buddies. I think fried turkey just may be a guy thing.

I have cooked a few traditional Thanksgiving dinners But that's not what my family remembers. Surprise, surprise, they remember my screw ups!

- One time I tried to make smoked turkey. I cut up the turkey before I brined it, smoked it, or cooked it. We had 12 pounds of turkey jerky.
- Another time we celebrated a Mexican Thanksgiving, I butterflied the turkey, rubbed it with lime juice and basted it with Tequila. Did you know that turkey can be tough, dry, and icky?
- I also smoked one turkey in very hot weather and it went bad. We had 14 pounds of foul, fowl. It was truly awful. I cooled this turkey, wrapped it in plastic and put it in a plastic bag. I tied it off, put it in a second bag and froze it until it could be hauled away on garbage day.

For the last few years I started soaking a turkey in salt-water instead of rubbing it with salt, pepper and spices. The finished turkey has skin that is not edible, but the turkey is moist, tender and delicious.

Dry Cure for Turkey

This recipe is from a co-worker Rich Rowe. It is easier than brining and the result is on a par with brining. I have used the same dry rub on a turkey breast and a whole chicken with excellent results.

Ingredients:

1 - turkey, 16 to 20 pounds (thawed)
½ cup packed brown sugar
¼ cup kosher salt
1 teaspoon garlic powder
1 teaspoon ground all spice
1 teaspoon ground cloves
1 teaspoon ground mace
2 teaspoons onion powder

Mix sugar and spices together until they are well blended. Rub the mixture over and under the turkey skin 24 hours before cooking. Store the turkey *uncovered* in the refrigerator for up to 3 days. Remove turkey from refrigerator. Pour off turkey juices and lightly rinse the turkey in cold water. Place turkey on a rack, breast side up and sprinkle with salt and freshly ground pepper. Preheat the oven to 350°. Cook turkey to an internal temperature of 170°. Allow it to set at least 20 minutes before carving.

The last time I made a dry-rubbed turkey breast I prepared a mixture using 2 tablespoons of light mayonnaise mixed with 1 ounce of blue cheese and 2 tablespoons of fresh chopped herbs. This mixture was inserted under the turkey breast. It improved an already good, good thing.

Great Cranberry Sauce, Also known as Drunken Cranberry Sauce

12 ounces fresh cranberries
1 cup sugar
2 tablespoons frozen orange juice concentrate
2 tablespoons Orange Liquor
the zest from 1 fresh orange

Directions:
Rinse the cranberries in cold water discarding any bruised or blemished berries.
Place the cranberries in an oven proof dish. Cover berries with sugar and stir in concentrate. Bake 1 hour at 350°. Remove from oven and stir in orange liquor and orange zest. This sauce tastes great and stores well.

TURKEY ROASTING TIMES @ 325 °

Turkey	Weight	Minutes/ pound	Total time	Temperature Breast	Thigh	Stuff ing
Unstuffe d	8 – 12	21 - 15	2 ¾ to 3 hrs	170°	180°	---
	12– 14	15 - 16	3 to 3 ¾ hrs	170°	180°	
	14 - 18	16 - 14	3 ¾ to 4 ¼ hrs	170°	180°	
	18– 20	14 - 13	4 ¼ to 4 ½ hrs	170°	180°	
	20– 24	13 - 12	4 ½ to 5 hrs	170°	180°	
	24– 30	12 - 11	5 to 5 ¼ hrs	170°	180°	
Stuffed	8 to 12	23 - 18	3 to 3½ hrs	170°	180°	165°
	12– 14	18 -17	3½ to 4 hrs	170°	180°	165°
	14 - 18	17 - 14	4 to 4 ¼ hrs	170°	180°	165°
	18– 20	14¼ -	4 ¼	170°	180°	165°

		14	to 4 ¾ hrs			
	20– 24	14 to 13	4 ¾ to 5 ¼ hrs	170°	180°	165°
	24– 30	13 to 12	5 ¼ to 6 hrs	170°	180°	165°

The internal temperature of the turkey will continue to raise 5° to 10° while the turkey rests before carving. Remove the turkey from the oven before it reaches the final temperature.

Many years ago someone started cutting up turkeys and selling them in pieces. Now turkey breasts, turkey cutlets, and ground turkey are available year round. I like turkey. I like it rubbed, brined and roasted. I don't trust ground turkey unless I grind it myself.

Substituting turkey for veal

Turkey Fillets with Pine Nuts
This recipe from the Ark Cookbook© is for veal. I made it with lots of substitutions, starting with turkey instead of veal. (Turkey is a fabulous substitute for veal!)

The following recipe reflects the changes I made. This goes together very quickly. I serve it with rice and a green salad. The flavors fit together very well. You will be surprised how good this is.

Ingredients:
4 turkey fillets (4 ounces each) cut from a whole turkey breast and pounded to about ¼ inch thick
1 tablespoon flour to dust the fillets
½ stick butter
2 tablespoons olive oil
2 cups sliced mushrooms
1 tablespoon chopped shallots
1 clove minced garlic
1 tablespoon fresh parsley, minced
¼ cup pine nuts, toasted
¼ cup red wine or raspberry-wine vinegar
1 tablespoon lemon juice.
1 tablespoon Dijon mustard.
½ cup Madeira or Marsala wine
¼ cup heavy cream
¼ cup chopped green onion

Directions:
Heat butter and oil in heavy sauté pan over medium high heat. Dust the fillets lightly with flour; shake of excess and sauté until lightly browned. Remove fillets to a heated dish. Add the next 6 ingredients to the sauté pan. Add vinegar, lemon juice, mustard, and marry well. Deglaze with wine, then add heavy cream. Reduce sauce until thickened then add green onions. Pour the sauce over the turkey fillets and serve.

Scaloppini *is usually made with veal*. Not this time.

This recipe is a good example
   2 boneless, skinless chicken breast halves
   or about 1 ½ pounds turkey breast
   1 tablespoon all-purpose flour

Salt and pepper
2 tablespoons or more of olive oil
3 tablespoons butter, divided
½ cup dry Marsala
½ lemon

Directions:

Cut each breast into fillets, 4 pieces for a chicken breast, or 8 pieces for a turkey breast, and pound until the cutlets are ¼ inch thick. Dredge the fillets in flour that has been seasoned with salt and pepper. Shake off all excess flour.

Heat the olive oil and 2 tablespoons of the butter in a large, heavy skillet. Add the fillets and sauté over medium high heat until fillets are golden brown on each side. Set browned fillets on a paper towel to drain. Deglaze the sauté pan with Marsala, stirring to loosen any browned bits until the sauce begins to thicken. Whisk in the last tablespoon of butter and remove from heat.

To serve, arrange fillets on a platter, cover with Marsala sauce and squeeze lemon over the top.

Simple Veal (Turkey) Francese

This recipe is from the Food Channel. The original recipe called for veal scallops from the calve's leg. It is another example of how turkey can be used in lieu of veal. This serves 2 people.

Ingredients:
½ pound turkey breast fillets
(in lieu of veal scallops from the calf's leg)
-salt and pepper
1 egg, well beaten
-Flour for dredging

6 tablespoons butter
1 cup white wine

Directions:

Place fillets between sheets of waxed paper and pound until thin, then season with salt and pepper. Place egg in a shallow bowl and place flour on a wide plate. Dip the meat pieces in the egg, then in the flour and set them aside.

Melt 4 tablespoons of butter over medium high heat in a sauté pan. When the butter foams, add the fillets. Sauté, until the pieces are golden brown then remove the fillets set aside. Add wine to the pan cook until reduced to ½ cup. Turn heat to low, add remaining butter and cook until thickened. Add the reserved meat pieces to the pan, turn them until they are coated with the sauce. Plate, top with remaining sauce and serve.

Turkey Picadillo – *This is a Cuban recipe.*

When I was a little girl, and I really got myself in a mess, my mother would say that I was in a pic-a-dillo. So, in American English it means fragmented or F'd up. In Spanish it means cut into small pieces. It is pronounced 'pick –a- Dee-yo'. I tried this, but added fresh red and yellow sweet peppers, substituted shallots for onions, and deleted the green olives. You can serve this as the meat portion of a nacho, with tortilla or corn chips, as a taco or burrito. They serve it with hot fried potato chips or with cooked peas and carrots.

Ingredients:

¼ cup raisins or other dried fruit, I like dried mangos
1 pound lean ground turkey
(*you can trust your butcher or grind the meat yourself*).
1 teaspoon ground cumin
1 teaspoon salt
1 teaspoon freshly ground pepper
1 tablespoon olive oil

3 garlic cloves, minced
1 small onion, finely chopped
1 tomato, peeled, seeded and chopped
10 green olives...I hate these things and won't use them
2 tablespoons drained capers plus 1 tablespoon caper brine
½ cup dry white wine
1 tablespoon tomato paste

Directions:

Simmer the dried fruit in ½ cup of water for about 10 minutes or until the fruit is plumped, soft and pliable and the liquid has been absorbed. Allow fruit to cool, then chop it into small sized pieces and set aside.

Combine turkey, cumin, salt and pepper in a bowl and mix well. Heat the oil over medium high heat in a heavy bottomed sauté pan or a cast iron skillet. Add the shallots, peppers and garlic and cook about 2 minutes or until vegetables are tender crisp. Add the turkey mixture and cook for another 2 minutes, stirring to break the mixture apart and incorporate it with the vegetables. Stir in the wine, tomato paste, fruit, and capers with reserved brine. Reduce the heat to medium and cook 6 to 8 minutes until turkey is done and most liquid has been absorbed. Correct the seasonings, adding salt, pepper or cumin as needed.

Add your favorite turkey recipes and notes here:

5. OTHER Feathered FOWL

If Chicken is the mainstay of our culinary lives, and it is.

And

If Turkey, the awkward flightless fowl, is a surprisingly versatile and incredibly inexpensive option, and it really is.

Then

It is at least possible that other birds could fly high at the dinner table. Some of these birds are wild-game birds and are only available to families with intrepid hunters. Others are readily available. These are the ones that come to mind:

Capon: A capon is a large castrated rooster that has been fattened for eating. It is generally slow roasted. In truth, I haven't seen one of these in a very long time.

Chukars: Chukars are small wild birds that run straight up steep hills. When they reach the top, they fly downhill. My husband brought some chukars home once after a day of hunting with his friend, Bill Friedlander. That was a long time ago, and I don't remember much about them. I think they were tasty. The breast was the only edible portion of the bird. The rest was full of buckshot and little dinky bones.

Cornish Hens: I used to make these pretty often. They were odd little birds, rather like undersized, abused orphans that invariably were missing a wing or a leg. Perhaps it was the lack of limbs that turned me off. Ron thinks Cornish hens are a waste of time. (He calls them worthless little f'ers) I don't like them very much either and I quit buying them years ago. There are lots of Cornish hen recipes. In my opinion virtually all of them are significantly improved by substituting chicken for the game hens.

Duck: In terms of cooking, there are three kinds of duck.

1. The beautiful wild duck: I find wild duck lovely to look at but tough, stringy and really dreadful to eat. Perhaps I need a better recipe.

2. Domestic duck: These ducks are frequently labeled 'Long Island Duck.' They can be found at most large grocery stores in the frozen food section. Unlike wild duck, the domesticated varieties are layered with fat. They are very rich, tender, and good.

3. Duck served in fine restaurants: There is a local, upscale restaurant, Tina's, that features at least one duck dish every night. My personal favorite is smoked duck breast with wild cherry or currant sauce.

Goose: On a cold autumn day long, long ago, Ron bagged a Canada goose. He cleaned and plucked it. I roasted it for Christmas dinner. It can't be as good as I remember it. Domestic goose is available commercially. Like domestic duck, it has thick layers of fat. It has been decades since my last roast goose dinner. If I remember correctly, it tasted like very fat roast beef.

Pheasant: These are beautiful birds. In the cornfields of central Illinois they are as common as mice. Like most wild birds, they work for a living; they are lean. Ron used to hunt pheasant. I remember roasting them slowly in liquid and serving them with a light cream sauce. Pheasant is not all that common where we live, but every once in a while we see a pheasant on the road. Ron hasn't hunted them since the early 70's. We both try not to cause pheasants any harm.

I have included a few fowl recipes:

Duck a La Orange

I use the recipe that comes on the frozen duck that is commercially available. It is very nearly foolproof and very good.

Caution: Domestic duck is very fatty, and the only worthwhile part is the breast. You will be shocked and amazed when you see how little edible meat you can glean from a 5 pound duck.

Duck Breast Winslade for Two
I am not sure where this recipe originated. But it's not difficult and it is pretty impressive. Fresh wild mushrooms are not critical, but they enhance the flavors and pair extremely well with the cranberries.

Ingredients
1 boneless, skinless duck breast, sliced lengthwise
¼ cup flour
½ teaspoon salt and pepper
2 tablespoon olive oil
1 tablespoon butter
½ cup or more, sliced fresh wild mushrooms
¼ cup dried cranberries
¼ cup rum
1 tablespoons honey
2 to 4 tablespoons ground almonds

Directions:
Cut the breast into 2 similar sized pieces. Remove skin, bones and all visible fat. Place the breast piece between 2 sheets of plastic wrap and pound until it is about ½ inch thick. Repeat this process with the other half of the breast. Dust the breast fillets with seasoned flour. Heat olive oil over medium high heat in a heavy bottomed non stick skillet. Sauté the duck fillets until lightly browned. This will only take 1 to 2 minutes per side.

Remove the fillets from the skillet and cover them to keep them warm. Add butter to the skillet. When the butter starts to foam, add the sliced mushrooms and cook them over high heat, stirring lightly until the mushrooms give up their liquid. Reduce the temperature to medium. Add the rum and cranberries to the skillet and cook stirring occasionally for 10 to 15 minutes. Add the honey to the skillet. Stir, to incorporate all ingredients, then pour the mixture over the duck fillets, sprinkle with ground almonds and serve.

This is something to consider when making this recipe:
I don't know where one finds duck breasts without the rest of their little fat bodies. When I made this dish, I started with a whole, frozen duckling. First, the breast was removed, skinned and boned. All visible fat was removed. This provided two halves of a duck breast which was a perfect start for the rest of this recipe. However, I also had the rest of the duck.

It was too expensive and too good to throw away. This was my solution: The mutilated remains of duckling along with the skin from the breasts were seasoned with salt and pepper then roasted at 400° in a shallow roasting pan for about 30 minutes. There was a deep layer of fat in the bottom of the roaster which was discarded.

However, we ate the 'cracklings' and we chewed the skin and knawed the meat off the duck legs. I made stock with the rest of the carcass and I even skimmed off the fat to make up for the cracklings binge. Duck cracklings certainly are not heart healthy, but they are Goooooood.

Warning! *If you have* <u>any</u> *Edwards's blood running through your veins, then you* **are** *subject to heart disease. That is just a fact of life. Discard my praise for cracklings. They could be lethal.*

Wild Game Birds:
I found a generic recipe for pheasant, grouse, sage hen, chukars or any upland bird. It comes from a wild game cookbook published by John Willard in 1958. This is it:

1. Kill the bird. Gut it and remove the head, feet and feathers.
2. Coat the bird liberally with butter, inside and out.

3. Make a stuffing from the heart, liver and gizzard mixed up with celery, onion, green pepper, a little sage, a dash of W. Sauce and a slice of orange. Stuff it inside the bird's cavity.
4. Wrap the bird in foil. Make sure the foil is sealed so no steam can escape.
5. Roast bird at about 400° for about 1 hour for a grouse or chucker, or 1¼ hours for a pheasant.

The author claims the result is too good for anyone but hunters or very honest men. Since I am neither, I haven't had an opportunity to try it.

Add notes here...

6. SEAFOOD: Fish - SWIM, SWIM

In Waukegan, 50 years ago, there were few opportunities to experience seafood. As a child, the closest I came to seafood was canned tuna fish and Mrs. Paul's Frozen (boneless) Fish Sticks.

Tuna noodle casserole and was a weekly entrée at my house on Butrick Street. 'Meatless Fridays' were a Catholic thing. The Edwards's on Butrick Street were definitely *not* Catholic. My family went to the First (and only) Presbyterian Church in Waukegan, Illinois.

Our church featured several concepts my father could accept:

- It operated as a democracy. The entire congregation was governed and led by the deacons and elders, not the minister. Dad was an usher, a deacon, and then an elder.
- The congregation was responsible for finding and hiring the minister. Dad considered him hired help. The congregation retained the right to boot the preacher out if he failed to meet expectations.
- There was one other thing Dad liked about the Presbyterian Church:

It Was Not Catholic.

Dad didn't dislike Catholics individually, but the idea of a ruling Pope left him a little crazy. Also, Catholic prohibitions at that time; Latin services, confession, birth control, and meatless Fridays - gave him all the ammunition he needed to blast them at will.

Ron gave me an engagement ring just before Christmas, 1963. When I broke the news to my dad he was underwhelmed. His plans for me included a college degree. The fact that I made the Dean's list didn't help. His grand-plan plan did not include some stump jumper. The other thing that didn't help was the name.

"Yasenchak, is he even an American?"

"Yes, he is."

"I suppose he's also Catholic." Right again. Dad was two for two.

Note: We did marry and are still together more than five decades.

Back to fish.

Mom liked fish, but she didn't prepare or serve it. The problem, besides availability, was Dad. Fish unfortunately have bones, sneaky little bones that are hard to see and even harder to swallow. Dad claimed to like fish (no one believed him) but he hated fish bones.

Occasionally Mom would find a fish that had been filleted so well that all bones were removed. She would cross her fingers and cook the fish. If Dad agreed to eat a piece of fish, he always ran across a bone and dinner morphed into a huge production.

It simply wasn't worth the trouble to even try to include fish in our diet. The one exception to the no fish rule was Mom's special tuna noodle caserole. She served this at least once every week, but never on Fridays. This recipe is here for historical reasons only. No one is required or even expected to make it. *It may not be entirely correct, but it's close.*

Grandma Mabel's Tuna Noodle Casserole

> 6 ozs. dried noodles
> 1 – 6oz. can of tuna packed in oil
> 1 – 12oz. can of Campbell's Cream of Mushroom Soup
> 1 small can of green peas
> Crushed potato chips for topping

Directions:

Boil noodles in salted water until soft. Drain and rinse. Mix the tuna, noodles, peas and soup together. Add a little milk to thin. Pour the mixture into a buttered casserole dish. Top with crushed potato chips, and bake for 30 minutes at 350°. The casserole should be hot and bubbly.

Fast-Forward to Fish in the Pacific Northwest: We eat fish three or four times a week.

My rules for purchasing fish are simple:
- Buy it at a fresh fish market
- Don't purchase prepackaged or frozen fish
- If there is a doubt regarding freshness, touch it and by all means, smell it.
- Consider this a hint: Fresh fish does not smell fishy.
- Don't overcook it.

Salmon

My first exposure to salmon occurred when we moved to Portland in 1970. In retrospect, it was not love at first bite. When I expressed my less than enthusiastic opinion, a native Oregonian explained that for some people salmon was an acquired taste. That could be true. If so, after all these years, consider me fully acquired!

I like salmon smoked, raw (in Sushi) broiled, grilled, baked, and poached. I have listed my three standby recipes for salmon, depending on the cut. I have also added some recipes that came from someone else.

Copper River Salmon: This Sockeye Salmon from the Copper River in SW Alaska may be the best salmon ever. This is fresh, *wild* salmon, not farm raised. Copper River Salmon has firm flesh and a deep red color. It's expensive and availability is limited. We get Copper River Salmon from the spring run, in May or early June.

Chinook Salmon: Chinook is also very good. It is found in Oregon streams and just off the Oregon and Washington coastlines. Chinook is surprisingly expensive considering the size, (large) and the numbers of fish available. We rarely see fresh Chinook in local fish markets. If you have a friend who will share his or her catch with you, that's a wonderful thing.

Steelhead: I used to confuse Steelhead with salmon. But they're not the same fish, not even the same species. Steelhead is in the trout family. I think of it as a trout on steroids. Unlike brook or brown trout, steelhead travel to the ocean and back. They can get very large, and pound for pound they are real fighters. The flesh is a dark pink. They are great fun to catch and darn good to eat.

We once found a steelhead on the beach. Apparently it had barely escaped a marauding seal, that had gouged a deep cut along it's flank. The fish jumped to eacape and landed on the sand. It was what one might call doomed. When we found the fish it was dead, but his eyes were still clear and he weighed about eight pounds. Ron cleaned and fileted it. I cooked it and topped it with the "Basalmic Maple Glaze" recipe listed on page 75.

It may sound a little like road kill – but It was delicious!

Other Salmon varieties: In addition to Chinook, we have Sockeye, King, Silvers, Chums and Pinks. There are probably others.

A notable exception:

The most abundant salmon is farm-raised Atlantic salmon. In my opinion it is inferior to anything we can find locally. Atlantic Salmon is better than canned tuna fish, but that's saying much. It is artificially dyed to look like real salmon. The flesh is soft and it lacks flavor. In my opinion it shouldn't even be considered the same species as Copper River.

My Recipes for Salmon

Fresh Salmon Fillets:
Preheat oven to 350°. Rinse the fillet with cold water and pat it dry. Place fillet skin side down on a piece of foil or a cookie sheet. Season the fillet with salt, pepper and fresh lemon juice. Frost the fillet with a thin layer of mayonnaise. Sprinkle the top with freshly grated parmesan cheese. Bake about 15 minutes per inch. The mayonnaise is just fat. It insulates the salmon and it keeps it moist. When the mayonnaise turns brown, the salmon is done.

Fresh Salmon Steaks:
Rinse steaks in cold water and pat dry. Dust the steaks with flour seasoned with salt, pepper and a little essence. Remove any excess flour and set the steaks aside. Add ½ tablespoon of butter and olive oil to a non-stick heavy bottomed sauté pan. Preheat sauté pan over medium high heat. Place fillets in the pan when the butter has melted and is just starting to foam. Do not crowd the steaks. Reduce heat to medium and pan fry until fish is lightly browned and flakes easily. The total cooking time will depend upon the thickness of the steaks. Remove the steaks and keep warm. If the oil/butter residue isn't scorched, add a little more butter, a dash of dinner wine. To serve, drizzle the wine mixture over the steaks, add a squeeze of fresh lemon juice and sprinkle with fresh parsley.

Whole Fresh Salmon
There are several options for whole fresh salmon:

Poached: Prepare poaching liquid using water and some chicken or vegetable stock. I usually add chopped onions, carrots and celery plus some fresh herbs to the stock. Place the salmon on a large piece of cheese cloth and gently lower it into the poaching liquid. Fish is done when it flakes easily.

Oven Roasted: Lightly salt and pepper the cavity and lay rosemary sprigs inside covered with fresh lemon slices. Place strips of bacon on top the salmon. Roast at 375° for 10 minutes per inch of thickness. When the internal temperature reaches 140°, the fish is done.

Barbecued, Ron's Method: Ron stuffs a whole salmon with lemon, onion slices and little gobs of tomato paste. He bastes the fish with lemon butter, wraps it in foil and then roasts it on the grill. This method cooks the salmon in its own juices. The finished salmon tastes great, but the flesh is more like that found in a poached fish.

Copper River Salmon with Balsamic Maple Glaze
If I ever knew exactly when I was going to die, I would request this dish for my last meal. I have made this many times. Use real maple syrup.   The glaze is good with any fresh, wild salmon, but it's fabulous with Copper River Salmon.

Ingredients:
¼ cup grapefruit or orange juice
¼ cup real maple syrup
3 tablespoons balsamic vinegar
2 cloves garlic, minced
4 tablespoon olive oil

4 - 5 to 6 ounce Copper River steaks or fillets
♦ salt and pepper

Directions:
Preheat broiler or grill. Combine the fruit juice, maple syrup, balsamic vinegar and garlic in a small sauce pan. Bring to a boil and cook, stirring often for 5 to 6 minutes or until sauce has a glaze-like consistency. Stir in the olive oil and remove from heat.
Season the salmon with salt and pepper and brush generously with glaze.

Broil or grill, basting often with the glaze, until cooked through, approximately 10 minutes per inch of thickness.

Cedar Plank Salmon:
The native Americans developed this method for cooking salmon fillets over on open fire
- They would soak a cedar plank in water for several hours.
- The plank would be covered with fresh herbs
- The salmon would be placed skin side down on top of the herbs.
- We use this method on our barbeque grill. The cedar adds a unique smoky flavor and the flesh is dry roasted rather than steamed inside a foil wrapping. We once prepared plank salmon with a fresh steelhead, the steelhead we found on the beach, and glazed it with the balsamic maple glaze shown in the previous recipe. It was so good.

Soy Lacquered Copper River Salmon with Green Onions
This recipe is influenced by the Shanghai style of Chinese cuisine. The light sauce compliments the perfectly poached salmon. I sampled this dish at the home of a professional cook book writer,

Dianne Morgan. It was wonderful! If Copper River Salmon is not available, substitute any firm, fresh wild salmon.

Ingredients:
½ cup soy sauce
¼ cup white vinegar
¼ cup granulated sugar
6 green onions, including green tops, cut into 1 inch pieces
6 to 8 quarter sized slices of peeled fresh ginger root, divided
4 – 6 ounce salmon fillets with pin bones and skin removed

To make the poaching sauce:
Combine the soy sauce, vinegar, and sugar in a small bowl. Stir until the sugar is dissolved. Add 4 of the green onions and half the slices of ginger root. Stir to coat the onions and ginger and set aside.

To poach the salmon:
Use a 10 inch sauté pan with straight sides to poach the fish.
Pour 2 cups of water into the pan, add the remaining 2 green onions along with the 4 remaining pieces of ginger. Bring the mixture to a boil, add the salmon fillets in a single layer and then reduce the heat so the water just simmers. Cover the pan and simmer the fish until it is barely opaque in the center. This will take 4 to 5 minutes depending upon the thickness of the fillets.

Use a small ladle to drain off all but ¼ cup of the poaching liquid. Remove and discard the green onions and ginger. Add the prepared sauce to the pan. Increase the heat to bring the liquids back to a gentle simmer. Baste the fish with the sauce and continue poaching about 4 minutes or until the fish is opaque or until it registers 125° on an instant read thermometer.

Remove the fillets from the pan and cover to keep warm. Increase the heat to medium high and boil vigorously to reduce the sauce. The sauce should thicken slightly but should not be syrupy.

To serve:
Have 4 entrée plates warmed and ready. If the salmon is being served with rice, arrange a flattened mound of rice on each plate. Place a fillet, flesh side up on the rice. Spoon sauce over the fillets and serve immediately.

Rosemary Roasted Salmon Fillet

We have fresh rosemary in our garden, and maybe it was just meant for this dish.

    2 large bunches fresh rosemary
    1 large red onion, sliced
    1 –2 pound center cut salmon fillet
    2 large lemons, thinly sliced
    1/3 cup olive oil

Directions:
Pre-heat oven to 500°. Arrange half the rosemary sprigs in a single layer in the center of a heavy baking sheet. Place the sliced onions on top of the rosemary. Place the salmon, skin side down on top the red onion. Sprinkle the salmon with salt and pepper then cover it with the remaining rosemary. Arrange lemon slices over rosemary. Drizzle olive oil over the top and roast the salmon until just it just cooked through. This will take about 20 minutes for a fillet 2 inches thick. If you want to be sure the salmon is fully cooked, check it with an instant read thermometer, and remove the salmon from the oven when the temperature reached 125°. Serve the salmon the roasted onions and some freshly sliced lemon.

OTHER FISH RECIPES

Salmon is my undisputed favorite fish, but we like a number of other varieties. For example, halibut is wonderful. It may be just as good as salmon. There are a few fish things I don't like:

- These include *bones*, especially the ones too small to see;
- heavy or greasy *breading*;
- *overcooked* fish;
- and the absolute worst, old *smelly* fish.
- I also have some personal, fishy beliefs:
- Sautéed or grilled fish is better than fried fish.
- Butter, citrus, wine and fresh herbs can make good fish better.
- A light flour dusting beats breading any day of the week.
- There is no reason to ever eat old or bad fish.

Tilapia:

This fish has been part of home aquariums for years. Large tilapia are raised in fish farms in South America and Africa. About fifteen years ago these farm-raised fish started appearing in local markets. My hard and fast rule to NEVER buy frozen fish was compromised regularly when it came to tilapia.

I found it to be a quality fish, inexpensive, and readily available. The small, (3 to 4 ounce) frozen, uncooked fillets were skinless and boneless. They had a pinkish color, but the cooked fish was white. The fish fillets froze well and lost little flavor in the process. The taste was similar to halibut but the texture was not as firm; more like sole. I absolutely recommended this fish. At home, I generally pan fried tilapia. My husband prefered it breaded with Panko crumbs. I was on a roll.

And then my niece Shelly gave me a lecture about Tilapia. She said they were raised in crowded, unsanitary ponds; and the small fillets were scavenged from damaged fish. She said they were disgusting! I believed her, and I promised her I wouldn't eat it again.

Orange Roughy with Pilonchillo

This recipe is from our friend, Gene Covey. Gene prepared this dish for us to illustrate that Mexican food goes far beyond the familiar Tex-Mex dishes. Gene perfected this recipe when he and Marcia lived in Mexico.

Ingredients:
1 Orange Roughy fillet per person
2 limes
up to 1 cube, 4 ounces of butter, divided
1 – 2 tablespoons flour
½ small papaya per person
¼ cup Pilonchillo: (pea-loan-chee-yo) This is raw Mexican sugar cane.

Directions:
Marinade fillets in fresh lime juice for 30 minutes. Use about 1 teaspoon of lime juice per fillet. Remove the fillets from the marinade, dry them off and then lightly dust each fillet with a little flour. Set aside. Peel the papayas and cut lengthwise into ¾ inch slices. Sprinkle the papaya slices with cinnamon. Use a large sauté pan or a flat griddle to cook this dish.

Fry the fish fillets in about 2 tablespoons of butter until browned and just done. Remove the fillets and place them on a heated platter. Add 1 more tablespoon of butter to the same pan and heat until the butter starts to foam. Sauté the papaya in the butter until just heated through. Place the papaya with the fish on the platter. Add a little more butter to the pan. As the butter starts to foam, add a tablespoon of lime juice and ¼ cup Pilonchillo to skillet. Heat until thickened. Place fish on a serving dish, surround with the papaya, pour sauce over fish and serve with rice.

Sole or Sand Dabs with Citrus

Sand dabs are little fish that live close to the shore. They are a tolerable exception to my no bones rule. They appear in the market very rarely. I think this recipe is good enough to substitute sea bass, halibut, monk fish, orange roughy, or any firm but delicate white fish. This recipe provides general guidelines – the list of ingredients is keyed to about one pound of fresh fish fillets.

> 4 - 4 to 6 ounce fillets
> ½ cup milk or half and half
> ¼ cup flour
> salt and pepper
> 2 tablespoons butter (divided)
> 1 tablespoon olive oil
> 1 medium sized orange, peeled, seeded and diced
> 1 medium lemon, peeled , seeded and diced
> ¼ cup dry white wine
> 2 tablespoons Triple Sec
> 1 tablespoon grated raw Mexican sugar

Directions:

Soak fish fillets in cream or milk for 30 minutes. Drain and dry the fillets then dust with seasoned flour. Combine 1 tablespoon butter and 1 tablespoon olive oil in medium-hot skillet. Add the fillets and sauté for 3 to 4 minutes per side. Remove the fillets from the pan and set aside. Add 1 tablespoon of butter to the pan. Add the pulp, diced, from 1 orange and the pulp, diced, from 1 lemon. Add 2 tablespoons of Triple Sec and ¼ cup dry white wine. Grate about 1 tablespoon raw Mexican sugar into sauce. Reduce sauce by 50% then add a scant teaspoon of raspberry puree. Cook until well blended. Pour sauce over the fillets and serve with hot rice.

Sturgeon:
Sturgeon is a fresh water fish. Locally, sturgeon are found in the Columbia River between Bonneville dam and the mouth of the river. They are very big, and while they are not pretty, the flesh from this ancient, bottom-fish is dense, rich and absolutely delicious when prepared correctly.

Sturgeon has a firm, unusual texture, similar to that of a land animal. When cooking sturgeon, test fish for doneness with your hand. The fillet will get firm around the outside part first. The firmer the fish; the closer it is to done. Use a non-stick heavy bottomed sauté pan. The fillets continue to approach the consistency of meat as they cook.

I have 3 recipes for sturgeon, all from the ARK Restaurant on Willapa Bay: Sturgeon Dijonnaise, Sturgeon with Garlic Raspberry Sauce and Sautéed Sturgeon with Wild Mushrooms. I have altered several ingredients. It is very important to have everything chopped, measured, and ready before you start cooking the fish.

Each recipe provides two servings and they all start the same:

- The fillets are cut into serving sized pieces, 3 to 4 ounces. The fillets are lightly dusted with seasoned flour and sautéed in hot clarified butter (or equal parts butter and olive oil) for 2 to 3 minutes, then turned over to finish cooking for another 2 to 3 minutes.

- Each recipe includes a variation of a cream sauce. The difference is in the accompanying ingredients that form the basis for the sauce.
- The Ark recommends serving sturgeon with hot white rice.

Sturgeon Dijonnaise: Heat a heavy bottomed 14 inch sauté pan over medium high heat. Add tablespoon of butter and a tablespoon of olive oil to the pan. Wait until the butter has stopped foaming then place the fillets in the pan. Continue cooking the fillets, but move them to the side and add following ingredients: ¾ cup sliced mushrooms, ¼ cup sliced onions, salt, white pepper to taste, a squeeze of lemon wedge and 1 dash of Tabasco. When the fillets are turned over, add ½ teaspoon minced garlic, 1 teaspoon Dijon mustard and 1/3 cup white wine. While fish cooks, add ¼ cup sherry, ¼ cup heavy cream and agitate to marry with rest of the sauce. Add 1/3 cup fresh diced tomatoes and 3 thinly sliced green onions.

Serve with white rice.

Sturgeon with Garlic Raspberry Sauce: The fillets are sautéed in hot butter, skin side up, for 2 minutes and then turned over. Add a squeeze of lemon, ½ teaspoon minced garlic, ½ teaspoon minced shallots and 1 tablespoon raspberry wine vinegar. Deglaze the pan with 3 tablespoons Madeira. Add 3 tablespoons raspberry sauce and 1 tablespoon cream. Allow to mix well. To serve, lace sauce over sturgeon. Garnish with fresh raspberries. Serve with white rice.

Sautéed Sturgeon with Wild Mushrooms: Sauté fillets skin side up in hot butter. Turn over. Add ½ cup sliced wild mushrooms, 1 teaspoon minced garlic, 1 teaspoon minced shallot, 1 teaspoon Dijon mustard, 1 dash Tabasco, 2 to 3 tablespoons fresh lemon juice, salt and pepper. With the fillets still in the pan, deglaze with a round of brandy, add 2 to 3 tablespoons fish stock and 1/3 cup heavy cream. Reduce briefly, then add 2 to 3 tablespoons of Madeira and reduce by one half. Check the texture of the fillet and the consistency, flavor and color of the sauce. Serve when fish is slightly springy to the touch and the sauce has a rich brown color.

Add your notes and favorite fish recipes here:

7. SHELLFISH

Shellfish is a generic term for crustaceans, aquatic animals with a hard shell. It is hard to believe that this collection of bottom feeders can provide such wonderful flavors. There are few rules to follow for successful preparation: The shellfish has to be fresh and it needs to be cooked quickly. Finally it needs to be showcased on it's own, not covered with excess sauces or breading. I buy shellfish from a fish market if possible. I want to see it, touch and smell it to be sure it is fresh. When I talk about shellfish, I am talking about the ones I particularly like to eat. These are:

Abalone: Abalone lives in warm waters off the coast of Southern California. The shell looks like a large scallop. The only edible or desirable part of the abalone is the hinge. Sometimes frozen abalone steaks can be found in an upscale fish market. The hinge has been pounded flat, and they are frozen in stacks. The individual steaks are about 4 inches in diameter and are separated by pieces of parchment paper. (I haven't seen these in years! Perhaps one has to be next to a warm ocean to find them.)

To prepare abalone, thaw the individual steak, dust it lightly with flour and sauté in clarified butter over medium high heat for about a minute on each side. Serve with a squeeze of fresh lemon and a dash of parsley. These are very rich. I would make one per person…maybe two. Sea otters love abalone, and they have almost wiped them out. The last time I saw abalone in a fish market was in the early 1980's. At that time, one dollar would buy three pounds of clams, and one pound of abalone cost $14.

Clams: The most common type of clam in the Northwest are the small butter clams, also called steamers. They are found in the sand at low tide along the Pacific coast. There are also larger razor clams and truly gigantic "geoduck" clams. If a person is willing to dig for clams, he will be rewarded with a bountiful variety. If not, the small steamers are usually available, and consistently good. We buy live, unopened clams. I scrub them to remove the sand. Then I place the clams in a mixture of wine, water, and spices that has been brought to a boil. The pot is covered and the clams are boiled only until the shells open. This takes 5 minutes or less. Discard any unopened shells. Dip clam in hot butter and enjoy.

Most restaurants in Oregon serve clam chowder. It's good. Costco has Jake's Clam Chowder® available in the can. They also have pouches of Ivar's Clam chowder® from the restaurants in Seattle. Both are as good as anything you can buy at the coast, and they are ever so easy to prepare. I think the best use of clams is as part of a medley in a fish soup or stew like Bouillabaisse, or Chiopino.

Razor Clams: *We recently found some fresh razor clams from Alaska at the market. The price was dirt cheap at $8 a pound. This is how I prepared them:*

- The fresh clams were rinsed in cold running water.
- They were dried with paper towels and cut into pieces.
- Anything that looks yucky was discarded.
- The pieces were dusted with seasoned flour, dipped into an egg wash, and then rolled in Panko crumbs.
- Finally I fried them quickly in hot vegetable oil.

These are fit for a God.
The next Razor clam recipe is from an upscale Portland restaurant and it is even better.

Wildwood Restaurant's Razor Clams
Wildwood was a Portland restaurant. Ron and I ate there as often as we could. I bought and frequently use their cookbook.

All of their meals and recipes are a delight to behold and a pleasure to eat. Razor clams are almost never available in a grocery store and they must be fried quickly. I have made some changes: This recipe called for meat tenderizer, toasted bread crumbs and polenta.

Disclaimer: *I never use or eat anything with MSG if I can avoid it. Polenta can be sometimes hard to find so I have substituted Panko for the coating.*

Ingredients:
12 fresh razor clams
1 cup fresh buttermilk
½ teaspoon kosher salt
¼ teaspoon black pepper
1 cup Panko bread crumbs
½ cup cornmeal
½ cup all purpose flour
Vegetable oil for deep frying
Tarter sauce

To prepare clams:
Spread the neck of razor clams and pound with mallet 4 or 5 times. Sprinkle clams with salt and pepper, then place in a shallow dish. Add the buttermilk to the dish and refrigerate for several hours. (I believe the step helps get rid of the sand...)

In a flat dish, stir together the flour, Panko crumbs, and cornmeal. Lift the clams out of the buttermilk. Let excess milk drain off. Dredge clams in a flour mixture and lay on a wire rack to dry for a few minutes.

Preheat oil in a deep pot or a wok to 375°. Fry the clams 2 at a time for 1 minute, then lift from hot oil with a slotted spoon and drain on paper towels. Allow the oil to reheat for a minute or two before adding more clams.

Serve these clams hot with tarter sauce, hot crusty French bread, red crab and a fresh green salad.

CRAB! In the northwest we have Dungeness crab and native freshwater crawfish. (Wasn't it nice of my grandson to pose for this picture!) There are lots of different kinds of crab; most of them are pretty good. When we first moved to Portland in 1970 Dungeness crab was a real bargain: 3 small or 2 large whole crab were sold for $1.

We considered it 'Poor man's lobster' and ate it at least once a week. I loved it.

If you find a friend that catches crab at the coast, be nice to that friend.

Encourage that friend to share his bounty. Crab cocktails, Crab Louis, hot crab sandwiches and crab bisque are all good. This recipe is just flat great.

Nick's Crab and Pine Nut Lasagna
I made this for our Christmas dinner in 2000. Fresh Dungeness crab and fresh lasagna noodles are pretty hard to beat. This slightly altered recipe is from Nick's Italian Restaurant in McMinnville.

Ingredients:
3 tablespoons butter
1 cup milk
1 cup half and half

3 tablespoons flour
1 teaspoon grated lemon peel
½ teaspoon roasted garlic
♦ salt and pepper to taste
½ pound **fresh** lasagna noodles
¾ pound Dungeness Crab meat
2 to 3 cups freshly grated Parmesan cheese
1 cup Ricotta cheese
1 to 1½ cups sliced mushrooms
¾ cup pine nuts

Directions:

Preheat oven to 375° Butter 9 x 13 inch pan. Set it aside. Boil lasagna noodles 2 to 3 minutes in large pot of boiling water then drain and rinse with cold water. Lay lasagna strips on clean towels and pat dry.

Make a béchamel sauce in a medium sized sauté pan. Melt 3 tablespoons of the butter, whisk in the flour, add the garlic and the lemon peel. Slowly whisk in the milk and bring to a boil. Then reduce the heat and simmer 3 to 4 min, season. Remove the skillet from the heat and set aside.

Cover the bottom of prepared pan with 3 cooked noodles.

Layer the crab meat over the noodles, placing one large piece of crab over each serving size piece.

Pour 2/3 cup of the béchamel sauce over the crab. Sprinkle with parmesan cheese.

Place a second layer of noodles over the cheese.

Cover the noodles with sliced mushrooms that have been lightly sautéed.

Add generous dollops of ricotta cheese over the mushrooms.

Spread béchamel sauce over the ricotta and sprinkle with parmesan cheese

Layer the remaining noodles over the parmesan cheese.

Spread béchamel sauce over noodles, top with parmesan cheese.
Sprinkle lightly browned pine nuts over the top.
Bake 30 to 40 minutes or until golden brown. Allow to set 10 minutes.

Lobster:

There is no way we can get truly fresh lobster in Portland. If I ever go to Maine, I will eat lobster. Monkfish is a firm white fish that is occasionally available in local markets. The fillets are shaped more like an overstuffed sausage than anything else. The fish is firm and sweet and can be substituted for lobster in recipes such as Lobster Americana and Lobster Newberg.

Mussels:

Mussels are closely related to clams. I think they are best steamed. This is my method:
Begin by running the mussels under cold water and scrubbing them to remove any unwanted debris, then set them in a colander to drain off the excess water.
Sauté about a half cup of onions, celery, garlic and carrots in a little olive oil. Cook until soft.
Using a stock pot, boil equal parts of water and white wine, add the sautéed vegetables, steam the scrubbed mussels until they open.
Mussels are delicious, but because they live at the edge of the water, and they can are subjected to pollutants. Both Ron and I have gotten very sick after eating mussels that smelled fresh and tasted wonderful. The next time I buy them I will really quiz the fish-monger.

Oysters:

Prior to moving to Oregon, I never considered eating oysters. For one thing, they look pretty weird. Another thing, the texture is suspect. Today, I really love fresh oysters either pan fried or steamed in the shell. If you pan-fry them, bread them in Panko crumbs. If you steam them, make sure they are fresh. Leave them in the shell and cook them quickly over a very hot grill. Serve these oysters with a knife to open the shell and some melted butter. Oysters have to be fresh, and I like them small. The big ones are just too gross.

Scallops:

There are two different kinds of scallops available. Large sea scallops are flown in from the gulf, (frozen) and much smaller bay scallops that (I think) are found off the Oregon coast. The small ones should be better, but they are absolutely inferior lacking both in texture and sweetness. Scallops need to be thawed, *dried* and cooked quickly. Overcooking makes them tough.

Chicken and Scallops with Tarragon (serves 2) Ark Cookbook©

2- 4oz boneless, skinless chicken breasts cut into 2 pieces
1 tablespoon butter
1 tablespoon olive oil
salt and pepper, Tabasco, squeeze of fresh lemon
½ teaspoon fresh chopped tarragon
2 or more cloves garlic, minced
¼ teaspoon chopped shallots
¾ cup sliced mushrooms
2 ounces fresh chicken stock
½ cup white wine
4 to 6 sea scallops
¼ cup heavy cream
2 tablespoons fresh parmesan cheese

Directions:

Heat butter and olive oil in a heavy, non-stick skillet over medium high heat. Sauté chicken pieces for two minutes on one side, then flip pieces over and cook just long enough to seal in the juices. Season with salt, pepper, Tabasco and a squeeze of lemon. Add the tarragon, garlic, shallots and mushrooms to the sauté pan and cook 2 to 3 minutes or until mushrooms wilt and shallots soften. Add the chicken stock and deglaze with wine. Add the scallops, heavy cream and parmesan cheese and cook for 1 to 2 minutes or until all ingredients come together. If the sauce takes more than a minute or so to thicken, remove chicken and scallops from the pan to avoid overcooking.

Place the sauce, chicken and scallops in a shallow oven proof casserole and sprinkle seasoned bread crumbs over the casserole mixture. Top casserole with freshly grated parmesan cheese. Bake at 425 ° for 8 to 20 minutes or until cheese is melted.

Shrimp: We can buy shrimp locally. The Oregon bay shrimp are very small, but they are inexpensive, fresh, and sweet. We use bay shrimp in salads, omelets and shrimp cocktails. All other varieties of shrimp come from the gulf coast or even further away. They may look fresh, but they're not. I would just as soon buy shrimp frozen, in the shell, and thaw them as needed. There are different kinds and sizes of shrimp available:

The very large fresh-water-shrimp look like a small lobster tail, but they don't have much flavor.

Tiger shrimp are full of flavor, but they run about 50 shrimp per pound. They need to be shelled and deveined: they are just too much work.

I prefer large salt water shrimp that are sold 15 to 20 per pound. I prepare about 4 to 5 shrimp per person. My favorite shrimp dish is simple: shell, devein, and butterfly the shrimp, flattening each shrimp with a cleaver for even cooking. Sauté shrimp in olive oil and melted butter over medium high heat. Add freshly chopped herbs, minced garlic and thinly sliced mushrooms to the sauté pan and cook with the shrimp. The shrimp are done when their translucent texture turns white. The dish is seasoned with salt, pepper and a dash of fresh lemon juice. It is served immediately.

Dilled Shrimp and Cheese Rolls

> 1½ cups cooked salad shrimp
> ¾ cup White Cheese, Monterey Jack or Swiss
> ¼ cup sliced green onions
> ½ teaspoon dill weed
> ¾ teaspoon salt
> 1/3 cup mayonnaise
> 1½ teaspoon white wine vinegar
> 6 sesame seed sandwich rolls, split and buttered

Directions:
Combine shrimp, cheese, onions, dill weed, salt, mayo and vinegar in a small bowl.

Spread the prepared sandwich rolls with the shrimp mixture. Wrap each roll individually in foil. Then bake in 350° oven for about 20 minutes.

Add your notes and favorite recipes here.

8. PASTA

We had two pasta meals at my house: Tuna casserole with noodles and Mom's Italian spaghetti. I don't remember when I first tasted lasagna or ravioli or any real pasta dishes. I'm sure it did not happen in Waukegan. I ate mom's spaghetti once a week, every Wednesday, for almost 20 years. I am pretty confident about this recreated recipe.

Grandma Mabel's Italian Spaghetti

    1 pound ground beef, broken into pieces and fried
    1 small onion, diced and added to the beef
    1 or 2 sticks celery, chopped and added to the beef
    1- 6 oz can tomato paste and 2 cans of water
    1-12 oz can of tomato sauce
    ♦   Salt and pepper to taste

Spaghetti: Boil some dried spaghetti, broken into pieces in salted water.
Cook until soft. Drain. Mix with meat sauce and serve.

When I first tasted fresh home made pasta with real Italian gravy I thought it was wonderful. The Italian gravy was what we call marinara sauce. It was made with fresh pork neck bones and real Italian sausage. When my Italian neighbor gave me the recipe for her gravy, and said it was easy to make pasta from scratch. I had to try.

In my first attempt, I made both the Italian gravy and the fresh pasta. I went to at least three stores for the ingredients. I also made 17 calls to my Italian friend, and I worked on this meal all day.

It was an unqualified disaster.

The pasta recipe called for flour, egg and water. The simple directions were to roll out the dough in small batches, cut it into thin strips, and then dry it prior to using it in a recipe. It may sound easy, but it wasn't.

I had pasta and flour all over our apartment. There were strips of dough hanging from the table, the countertops, lampshades, and every chair. There were strips of pasta hanging EVERYWHERE. I didn't roll the dough thinly enough. When I cooked the strips, God help me, I tried several different batches. None of them were edible. The pasta strips either disintegrated or clumped together in an unpleasant mass.

Now, let me tell you about the gravy. First, I had to find pork neck bones.

Between the pasta fiasco, and picking pork bones out of the sauce, I gave up making authentic Italian gravy. Today, I use Ragu® or an improved version of Ragu® and I buy fresh pasta. For the sake of posterity, I felt compelled to include the recipe.

<u>Real</u> Italian Spaghetti

Ingredients:
3 pounds pork neck bones
Olive oil
Tomatoes, fresh, or canned or stewed… Lots of tomatoes
Lots of fresh parsley, chopped
Fresh garlic, crushed and minced
Water
Red wine
- Fresh Italian sausage

- Fresh homemade pasta

Directions:
- Brown the neck bones in hot oil
- Place browned bones in a large stockpot.
- Add (skinned) tomatoes, garlic, a handful of chopped parsley,
- salt and pepper, and 1½ to 2 cups of water.
- Simmer uncovered for an hour or so, until the meat starts falling off the bones and the broth thickens.
- Check for seasonings.
- Add wine, more parsley and a little more water.
- Remove the pork neck bones, cool them and attempt to pull all the meat off the bones. Discard the bones.
- Brown the sausages. Cut into 2 or 3 inch pieces. Add to sauce.
- Simmer another 30 minutes or until sausage is done and sauce is thick.
- Serve over freshly made, cooked pasta.
- Top with freshly grated Parmesan Cheese.

Other Pasta Recipes

When I was still working, I bought a lot of box mixes of fettuccini, vermicelli, etc. These dishes were all right, mostly they were cheap, fast and very easy. Now that I have more time, I can be a little more selective. I've found that fresh pasta is better than dried.

Pasta with Creamy Ricotta Pesto
This recipe is from Bon Appetite's series for people who are 'Too busy to Cook.'©

Ingredients:
¾ cup fresh basil
¼ cup fresh parsley

1 clove garlic
¼ cup olive oil
1 cup ricotta cheese
1 pound fettuccine freshly cooked
1 pint fresh cherry tomatoes
Freshly grated parmesan cheese

Directions:
Mince basil, parsley and garlic in food processor or blender. Add oil, process until thick, about 10 seconds. Add ricotta and process until well blended. Arrange pasta on serving platter. Pour pesto over pasta and toss to coat. Top with tomatoes. Serve, pass cheese separately.

Carbonara, Quick and Easy

Ingredients:
8 slices of thick bacon, cut in 1 inch pieces
½ cup whipping cream
1 teaspoon red pepper flakes
3 eggs, beaten to blend
1 cup freshly grated parmesan or Romano cheese
½ pound dried linguini freshly cooked
¼ cup butter, melted
♦ Salt and freshly ground pepper

Directions:
Cook bacon over medium heat until crisp. Remove with slotted spoon. Pour off all but 1 tablespoon of the drippings. Add cream and pepper flakes to skillet, heat until warm, 3 to 4 minutes. Whisk eggs and ½ cup parmesan cheese in small bowl.

Place cooked pasta in serving bowl. Add heated butter and toss. Stir in egg mixture, add cream mixture, and toss thoroughly. Mix in bacon.

Season with salt and pepper. Sprinkle with remaining parmesan cheese.

Fettuccine Alfredo

Ingredients:
1 pound fresh fettuccine
6 tablespoon butter
2/3 cup whipping cream
½ teaspoon salt
freshly ground black pepper
1 large piece freshly ground nutmeg
1 cup fresh grated parmesan cheese
2 tablespoons fresh parsley for garnish

Directions:
Cook fettuccine according to package instructions, do not overcook.
Melt butter in a heavy skillet over medium heat. Add cream, salt, pepper and nutmeg.
Gradually add cheese, do not boil.
Ladle over hot fettuccine – Serves 4 to 6.

Spaghetti Pie...You really have to try this.
I found this recipe in Food Day. It is amazing. Of course, I modified it. The first time I made it we darn near licked the bowl. The last time I made it I used too much marinara sauce and probably too much cheese. It was sloppy, the spaghetti crust was goopy... I recently gave this one more try. I followed the recipe more carefully. It was really, reallly good.

Ingredients:
8 ounces hot cooked **fresh** angle hair spaghetti, drained
2 tablespoons olive oil or butter

2 eggs, well beaten
½ cup plus 2 teaspoons freshly grated asiago cheese, divided
1 cup part skim ricotta cheese
1 cup spaghetti sauce
½ cup grated mozzarella cheese

Directions:
Preheat oven to 350°. Lightly grease a 10 inch pie plate. Set aside.
In a large bowl, toss hot spaghetti with olive oil. Pour spaghetti
mixture into pie plate, spreading to form a crust.
In a small bowl beat the eggs, add the ricotta cheese and half of the
parmesan cheese, stir, Spread ricotta mixture evenly over the crust,
but not quite to the edge. Top with spaghetti sauce.
Bake uncovered 25 minutes.

Top with mozzarella cheese and bake 5 minutes longer or until
cheese melts. Remove from oven and sprinkle with remaining 2
tablespoons of parmesan cheese. Cool 10 minutes before cutting
into wedges.

Wide Noodles with Basil Ricotta
*This may sound like dorm food, ground beef and noodles. Don't be
fooled. It is better.*

Ingredients:
1 – 15 oz container of part-skim ricotta cheese
1/3 cup chopped fresh basil
½ t. salt
1 T. olive oil
1 medium onion, chopped
2 cloves garlic, minced
1 pound extra lean ground beef
½ cup hearty red wine (Red Zinfadel)

1– 28 oz. can crushed tomatoes in puree.
1– 14 ounce can diced tomatoes in juice
2 teaspoons dried oregano
1 pound fettuccine or pappardelle noodles
 ♦   freshly grated parmesan cheese for serving

Directions:

Mix the ricotta, 1/3 cup basil and salt in a medium bowl. Let stand at room temperature while you prepare the pasta. (Ricotta will lose its chill)

Heat olive oil in a large skillet over medium heat. Add onion and cook, stirring occasionally until softened. Add garlic, cook 1 minute. Add ground beef, increase heat to medium high and cook, breaking up with a spoon until meat loses its pink color, (about 5 minutes.) Add the wine and bring to a boil.

Stir in crushed tomatoes, diced tomatoes with their juices and the oregano. Return to a boil then reduce heat to medium low. Simmer uncovered until sauce thickens, about 25 minutes.

Meanwhile, boil salted water in a large pot. Add pasta. Cook until barely tender, about 9 minutes. Drain pasta and return to pot.

Add sauce to the pasta and mix well. Serve immediately in individual bowls. Top each serving with a large spoonful of the basil ricotta and a sprinkle of chopped basil. Pass parmesan cheese on the side.

Notes:

9. RENAISSANCE – A Rebirth or Revival
The art of turning "Left-Overs" into Artful Creations

My husband calls these recipes "Becky's Do-Overs."
Ron doesn't like to talk about them; he does enjoy eating them.

This is the art of turning "Left-Overs"
Into *Artful* Creations.
There are three secrets:

1. Use your imagination!
2. Reheat, don't re-cook the leftover
    food.
3. Disguise the new dish with fresh, new ingredients.

Left Over Food:

When I was a child, left-over food had a bad reputation. In
Waukegan we called left-overs "Garbage!" We might feed this food
to the dog. Especially if we didn't like the dog.

I inherited my parents' reluctance to waste food. My husband
brought with him a distain for left-overs. I had to find a way to
disguise the second coming of a prior meal.

At my house we didn't waste much. Mom was thrifty; Dad was
cheap. Some items that would have been quickly discarded in other
homes were saved or salvaged. In terms of food, Dad had first and
last choice of all food served at any meal. If there was anything left
in a serving dish, Dad would look at it and say:

"Does anyone want any more of this?"

We all understood that asking that question was in no way an invitation to eat more. If Mom made something really special, we might ask for a second helping. Mom's most common response to that type of request was: "No. You've had enough."

All leftover food was for Dad. If Dad didn't want it, or if he didn't eat all of it, Mom had the option of throwing it away or saving it.

It was hard, almost impossible for mom to throw away perfectly good food. Mom called these leftovers 'smidgens.' She would save a 'smidgen' of mashed potatoes, or steak or a half piece of pie.

In the 1950's Tupperware© had not been invented, but we had aluminum foil. The 'smidgen' would be formed into a sort of ball, wrapped in foil, and placed in the refrigerator. At the end of three or four weeks the refrigerator would be littered with little clusters of foil bundles, here, there and really everywhere.

None of the foil packets were ever labeled. I suppose my mom had some idea what was there. We didn't and no one was brave enough to go surfing through a cold aluminum jungle. Thank God refrigerators had to be defrosted! About once every 6 weeks Mom would defrost the refrigerator and threw away those semi-precious bundles. Smidgens were not garbage, but if they were hidden away long enough they could and frequently did become garbage.

The following food items were deemed 'garbage' and could go straight to the garbage can:

- **BBR** (Burned Beyond Recognition) foods
- **Anything Dad Didn't Like:** If dad didn't like it, it couldn't be good.

- **Technicolor Foods:** Food that has overstayed its welcome and changed from its original color to green, blue, pink, white or hard yellow.
- **Colorful Colonies:** Truly outdated food was usually found in a plastic container. Cottage cheese is a good example. Geriatric cottage cheese, left alone long enough, could easily qualify for a lab experiment. It passed the garbage test.
- **Rock Hard Food:** Some foods don't get soft and nasty. Instead, they lose all their moisture and become hard. Cheddar Cheese is a good example of this phenomenon. If the food item was too hard to bite into, or if it bounced or broke into pieces when dropped, it qualified as garbage and could be discarded.

All other foods were proclaimed 'perfectly good.' You can trust me on this: 'Perfectly Good' **_NEVER_** meant perfect and rarely meant good.

When I got married I started cooking, I thought I was a pretty good cook. I was wrong. Every meat dish I prepared was laced in one way or another with onions and/or tomatoes. The acid from the tomatoes and gas from the onions were very hard on my young husband's digestive system. In less than 6 weeks he had a full-blown ulcer. After years of living quite nicely on dormitory, cafeteria and fast food, I was killing him with love and my version of home cooking.

Ron's doctor prescribed antacid pills and Maalox® tablets for Ron. Then he lectured me about my cooking. He *strongly* suggested that the meals I prepared conform to the soft, bland food my husband needed to get well.

At the time I didn't even own a cookbook. The idea of reading and closely following the directions found in proven recipes was an alien concept.

Ron bought me my first cookbook with highlighted recipes for me to try. Time passed. His ulcer healed. I bought more cook books and tried many new recipes. In time, and with a lot of practice, I became a pretty good cook but I almost always made too much food. When our children were little, Ronda ate few vegetables and little meat. She loved junk food and shunned almost everything else. David didn't like vegetables either, but he did like meat, cheese and sandwiches. As long as David and his friends lived with us, too much was just about right. A large roast would provide one big meal and enough sandwiches to get three teenage boys through the evening.

When our kids left home for good, Ron started cooking with me. We tried a lot of different recipes using exotic and often expensive ingredients. The meals got better.

But even when a dish was incredibly good, we rarely ate all of it. Ron still didn't want anything 'left over.' His solution was feed whatever was left to the dog, or to throw it in the garbage. For a while, the dog was in pig heaven. Then, our dog died. This created a new dilemma.

There was always excess food. It was way too good, and I was too cheap to consider it garbage. It simply didn't meet the strict garbage criteria that had carried over from my childhood. My husband could have lived with an expanded version of the Edwards Garbage Criteria, but I couldn't. I tried several different approaches:

- I tried just heating it up and reserving it. In truth, what was tender and succulent on day one was frequently dried out, overcooked and completely lackluster on day two. It is almost as if the second coming was purposefully poor so whatever was still available could be thrown out with a clean conscience.

- I searched for recipes that featured 'cooked' meat, like fried rice or pot pies. In time, I found a way to resurrect those meals in such a manner that even Ron accepts them graciously and he no longer complains…well he sometimes complains.

The secret to culinary success (a day or two later) is to create a disguised or *renaissance* version of a memorable feast. This requires a bit of imagination, a few new ingredients and a very short cooking time. The following food categories are not really recipes, they are suggestions of what could and might be done with excess food.

Beef: When I say beef, I generally mean beef from an expensive, tender cut that was cooked medium rare the first time around. The trick is to heat it through but not cook it any longer. It sounds like a delicate balance, but it's not hard to do.

Beef Bar-B-Que: Prepare a basic barbeque mixture or use something that has been commercially prepared. Sauté chopped onions or shallots with a little olive oil in a sauté pan over medium, high heat. Add the bottled barbeque sauce with a little water, and let the sauce cook down. Add thinly sliced beef roast to the mixture. Heat through very quickly and serve immediately.

Beef Fajitas: Prepare the onions, peppers, tomatoes and any other vegetables for the fajitas. Sauté the pared vegetables in a little olive oil over medium high heat, seasoning them with cumin, salt and pepper. Add thinly sliced strips of beef to the onion/pepper mixture right before serving. The meat will pick up the heat and flavor of the vegetables and spices while retaining its tenderness. The resulting fajitas are better than good.

Beef Miroton: This is a classic French recipe that combines leftover beef and potatoes in a casserole. The cold potatoes are sliced and layered along the inside edge of the dish. The beef is sliced paper thin and placed in the center. The casserole is topped with a sautéed mixture of sweet onions, red sweet pepper and diced pickle. Fresh breadcrumbs are spread over casserole and it is baked in a hot oven for about 20 minutes.

<u>Becky's</u> Beef Miroton

I found a new French recipe for left over steak or rare roast. I remembered that I used to make beef miroton quite a bit. That was long before our son, David, began devouring all available meat at every single meal. By the time he left home, I had all but forgotten all about left-over anything.

This is my recipe for Beef Miroton from long ago, when I was thrifty. It is the way I remember Beef Miroton, and I think it is better. Now that Ron and I are the only ones here, I think I will try it again! If this sounds like something you would like, you should try it in the near future, before someone in Washington DC adds catsup to it and renames it American Beef Miroton.

Ingredients:
1 tablespoon olive oil
1 tablespoon butter
1 medium sized onion, minced
¼ cup red wine vinegar
½ cup bread and butter pickles
1 tablespoon tomato paste
1 to 1½ pounds leftover rare steak or roast
3 or 4 medium sized boiled or baked potatoes, peeled and sliced ¼ inch thick

½ cup grated Swiss cheese
½ cup bread crumbs made from day old French bread

Directions:

Place olive oil and butter in a heavy bottomed sauté pan or a cast iron skillet. Heat over medium high until butter is hot but not smoking. Reduce the heat to medium, add the onions and cook until they are translucent and just beginning to caramelize. Add the vinegar, pickles and tomato paste. Cook, stirring gently until all ingredients are incorporated, then remove skillet from the heating surface.

Butter an oven proof baking dish. Layer the potato slices around the outside of the dish. Place the thinly sliced roast beef in the center of the dish. Cover the beef with the onion/pickle mixture. Sprinkle the buttered bread crumbs and cheese over the meat and potatoes. Bake in a 350° for oven for 25 minutes or until cheese melts and beef is hot.

Beef Sirloin Tips in Peppercorn Gravy:

This recipe is for left over steak. Cut the cold steak into bite sized chunks and set aside.

To prepare the gravy, I recommend a pre-packaged brown gravy mix. Away from the heat source, pour ½ cup cold water into a small sauté pan and add the powdered gravy mixture and stir. When the lumps have disappeared, place the sauté pan over medium heat and cook, stirring until gravy starts to thicken. Instead of adding the rest of the water, substitute ½ cup of sour cream and cook mixture for a minute or so. When the cream has been incorporated and the gravy is simmering, add the drained peppercorns and the pieces of left over steak. Heat through quickly and serve with mashed potatoes.

Crepes:

Crepes are little pancakes filled with something, almost anything, then topped with a sauce and baked until hot. There are a couple of critical tips:

Basic Crepe Batter, with Fresh Herbs

I adapted this recipe from the Wildwood Cookbook. It makes thin, very delicate, delicious crepes. There are 3 critical tips to insure a perfect result every time: Let the crepe batter "rest" in the refrigerator for at least an hour before making the crepes. Have all ingredients cut, diced and divided before you cook the crepes. Use a teflon pan with a flat surface to cook crepes. The crepes can be filled with almost any left over beef, pork, chicken or fish and covered with a light sauce.

Crepe Ingredients:

1 cup milk
1 large egg
3 tablespoons butter, melted and cooled to room temperature
¾ cup all purpose flour
¼ cup finely minced fresh tarragon, chives and flat leaf parsley

Directions:

Before making the crepes, stir the batter to insure even consistency. Cook crepes quickly, one at a time. Place a 7 to 9 inch Teflon sauté pan over medium high heat. Coat the pan with non-fat spray. Ladle ¼ cup of batter into the pan tilting the sauté pan to cover the cooking surface. Cook crepe for 1 to 2 minutes or until it is lightly browned. Flip the crepe over cook other side for 30 seconds. Turn out on a kitchen towel and allow to cool.

Omelets:
See egg section for hints and examples of omelets.

Pasta with left over meat:
Adding leftover chicken, turkey, pork, even beef to fresh pasta is a wonderful way to enjoy leftovers instead of throwing them away.

Roll ups:
These are flour tortillas that are filled with tasty concoctions and can be served as a wrap type sandwich or can be rolled up and then sliced as an appetizer. *These are general guidelines*:

- Lightly frost tortilla with mayonnaise, or cream cheese, or salad dressing, or chutney or a relish. Use your imagination. Almost anything will suffice.
- Layer the tortilla with slices of meat, or cheese, or spinach or roasted peppers or whatever your refrigerator and imagination can agree upon.
- Roll the tortillas and cover them with plastic wrap. Refrigerate, seam side down, for 2 or 3 hours or overnight. To serve, remove the wrapping and slice in ¼ to ½ inch slices.

The first time I had rollups they were filled with a spinach dip and some minced crumbled bacon. Today I make these with anything and everything. My most surprisingly good variation involved cream cheese, turkey slices and drunken cranberry sauce.

Salads:
Leftover meat can turn an ordinary salad into a meal. See salad section for some examples. I think my favorite meat salad is rare roast beef salad.

Salmon Cakes

At one time I made salmon cakes with a 16 ounce can of salmon. I still use canned salmon occasionally, but it is not really necessary. You don't need canned salmon. You don't need canned anything. You can substitute almost any kind of left over fish and turn it into a fish cake.

And a true Renaissance recipe.

> 1 – 16 ounce canned salmon (or left-over cooked salmon)
> 1 egg, beaten
> ½ teaspoon salt
> ½ tablespoon freshly squeezed lemon juice
> 1½ tablespoons mayonnaise
> 2 or 3 minced green onions
> 1 tablespoon fresh dill or other herb of choice
> ½ cup of Panko
> 1 tablespoon butter

Prepare the canned salmon by draining off all liquids and removing all skin and bones. There will be about a cup of usable salmon. Place the salmon in a small bowl. Add the beaten egg and stir, then add the rest of the ingredients listed and mix gently until all ingredients are evenly distributed. Form the mixture into 4 to 6 cakes. Melt butter in a heavy bottomed non-stick sauté pan. When the butter starts to foam, add the fish cakes to the pan and sauté over medium heat until the cakes are lightly browned.

I use left-over salmon for a breakfast treat. I make the fish cakes, top each cake with a poached egg, and serve it with hollandaise sauce. It is spectacular.

10. APPETIZERS:

In Waukegan, food was breakfast, lunch or supper. People who lived in our part of town went 'out' for dinner. My mother occasionally served appetizers to special guests. Dad called these pre-meal tidbits "Whore De Or vies."

Do snacks fit into the same category as appetizers? If they do, I will mention that the only snack food at our house was popcorn. My dad rarely spent much time in the kitchen, but he assumed total responsibility for popping corn. Dad had a designated three quart popcorn pan. He never measured anything, but he had an uncanny ability to accurately estimate the correct amount of popcorn. He never scorched the pan and there were almost never any 'old maids.

I still remember how he made popcorn: He would melt a little Crisco® in his special pan, then he would add just enough pop corn to almost cover the bottom of the pan. The next step was to cover the pan and bring the popcorn to temperature. When the first kernel popped, Dad would move the pan back and forth across the burner. He would continue this action until the cacophony of popping kernels slowed and the lid to the pan pulled away from the rim. Dad would dump the finished popcorn in a big mixing bowl.

He drizzled some melted Imperial® margarine over the top and added quite a bit of salt. It was heavenly. Sharon and I loved Dad's popcorn, but we rarely had an opportunity to indulge ourselves in this special treat. Invariably Dad would make popcorn after we had been banished to our rooms for one infraction or another. We would be upstairs, commenting on how ludicrous and unfair life was. The next thing we knew, the unmistakable smell of popcorn would come wafting up the stairs.

Sharon and I would quietly creep back down the stairs. I have no idea why we even tried because Dad would never give in. There was never any popcorn for bad little girls.

The only appetizers I can remember are deviled eggs, raw carrots, cut up celery and little cocktail wieners. I remember there was a bakery in Waukegan that dyed white-bread red, green and/or yellow. Mom liked to make made little sandwiches filled with tuna or ham or egg salad for the Ladies Guild and other functions at the church. The sandwiches could be made in advance and they were both colorful and tasty. This is the recipe:

Mother's Festive Little Sandwiches

1. Purchase one or more loaves of baked white sandwich bread that has been dyed pink, green or yellow. This specialty bread is sliced in a horizontal rather than vertical manner. There are 4 long rectangular slices in each loaf.
2. Trim off all crusts. Separate the slices. Spread prepared sandwich filling on the entire length of each slice.

Spiral sandwiches: Roll the bread slice, filling side up, jellyroll style. Wrap in saran wrap and refrigerate until ready to use. To serve, cut the jelly rolled sandwiches into ¾ inch slices and place on a pretty plate with a little parsley for garnish.
Stacked sandwiches: Stack the prepared bread slices. Cut into squares, 4 x 4. Wrap in saran wrap and refrigerate until ready to use. To serve, cut each square into 4 rectangular pieces and place on a pretty plate with a little parsley for garnish.

Mom would usually have at least 2 loaves of colored bread and 3 different sandwich fillings. She would try to coordinate the colors.

For example she might put egg salad with the green bread. These little sandwiches were attractive, tasty and a big hit.

Necessary notes: You may have to go to Waukegan to find this colored bread. Today, lucky us, we have flour tortillas that are available in different flavors and colors. In my opinion, tortillas really are the greatest thing since, well, sliced bread.

Mom and Dad moved to Arizona when they retired in 1965. In Arizona, Mom had more time and opportunities for appetizers than she ever had in at our home in Waukegan. The following 3 recipes are taken from her 1970's hand written cook book.

Party Turnovers

> 1 envelope Lipton's Onion Soup Mix®
> 1 pound ground beef
> 1 cup shredded cheddar cheese
> 3 packages refrigerator crescent rolls
> Preheat oven to 375°

- Brown ground beef in a medium sized skillet over medium high heat. When the beef has lost most of it's color, stir in the soup mix and continue cooking for a minute or two then add the cheese.
- Remove the skillet form the heat and set aside.
- Separate the crescent rolls according to package directions and cut each roll in half.
- Place a spoonful of the meat mixture on each triangle, fold it over and seal edges.
- Place the rolls on a cookie sheet and bake for 15 minutes.
- This recipe makes 48 turnovers.

Teriyaki Meatball Fondue

This recipe had my name on it. I don't remember this recipe, but my husband says it was part of my repertoire when we first moved to Portland in 1970. You will need a fondue pot and a supply of fondue forks.

Ingredients:
1 tablespoon soy sauce
1 tablespoon water
2 teaspoons sugar
½ teaspoon minced onion
1 clove garlic, minced
½ pound ground steak
½ cup soft bread crumbs
1 cup or more vegetable oil for cooking.

Combine the soy sauce, water, sugar, onion and garlic in a small bowl and set it aside.

Use a separate bowl to mix ground steak and bread crumbs together. Combine steak mixture with the soy mixture and form into ¾ inch balls.

Heat oil in fondue pot until it is very hot. Spear the meatballs with fondue forks and cook in boiling oil for 2 minutes or less.

I don't make appetizers very often for 3 very good reasons:

1. My husband thinks the whole idea of eating before you eat is silly. He may be right.

2. In order to prepare appetizers it takes planning, work and forethought. Not my style.

3. I really like appetizers. so when we do have them I eat too much or too many.

However, in spite of these three good reasons, we still have appetizers or snacks in lieu of a meal. These occasions are truly a spur of the moment decision.

- There are truly wonderful cheeses and my husband and I like them all. I think they should be declared a special food group along with wine and chocolate. Anyway, good cheese with crispy crackers and a glass of wine is a fine appetizer.
- Smoked salmon, especially with cream cheese and crackers is pretty tasty.
- Cold boiled shrimp with cocktail sauce is also nice.

Sometimes one has to work a little harder. I find the following recipes for appetizers worth the effort and the calories:

Cold Crab Appetizer

Ingredients:
½ pound Dungeness crab
½ tablespoon fresh lemon juice
2 tablespoons olive oil
2 to 3 tablespoons fresh minced herbs
♦ salt and pepper to taste
1 tablespoon minced shallots
¼ cup mayonnaise

Directions:
Toss the crab with lemon juice, oil, salt, pepper, shallots and herbs, then let the mixture stand 20 minutes to absorb flavor of seasonings. Drain off most of the excess liquid, then toss with mayonnaise to lightly coat crab. Serve over a bed of salad greens with crackers.

Cheese Straws
There may be an easier appetizer, but I doubt it.

1 pound puff pastry, thawed
¾ cup fresh grated parmesan cheese

Directions:
Roll pastry into a 20 x 24 inch rectangle. Press in half the cheese. Fold the dough in half and roll out a 20 x 24 inch rectangle. Press in balance of the cheese. Cut the dough into ½ inch strips and twist strips into cork screw. Bake at 350° for 15 to 20 minutes. Cool 5 minutes, then break apart. Store in an air tight bag.

Dilled Shrimp and Cheese Rolls
I think I found this old recipe from Sunset Magazine© circa 1970. It is really GOOD! In the old days we had to heat these in the oven and it took about thirty minutes. Today, we have the option of cutting the heating time to about one minute in the microwave. If you choose to do that, be careful to keep the buns from turning into latex.

Ingredients:
1½ cup cooked salad shrimp
¾ cup white cheese, Monterey Jack or Swiss
¼ cup sliced green onions
½ teaspoon dill weed
¾ teaspoon salt
1/3 cup mayonnaise
1½ teaspoon white wine vinegar
6 sesame seed sandwich rolls, split and buttered

Directions:

Combine the shrimp, cheese, onions, dill weed, salt, mayo and vinegar in a small bowl.

Spread sandwich rolls with the shrimp mixture then wrap each roll individually in foil. Bake the rolls in a in 350° oven for about 20 minutes.

Blue Cheese Log

This recipe is from Dorothy Patrick. She is a good friend and really a good cook.

Ingredients:

4 tablespoons sesame seeds
2 teaspoons butter, melted
2 - 8 oz. packages cream cheese
4 ounces blue cheese
1 cup shredded cheddar cheese
1 tablespoon Worchester sauce
¼ teaspoon onion powder
♦ a pinch of garlic powder

Directions:

Toast sesame seeds in a non-stick sauté pan over medium high heat until light brown. Remove the pan from heat and set it aside.

Melt butter in the microwave in a glass pie plate for 30 to 45 seconds and set aside.

Place the cream cheese, blue and cheddar cheeses in a 2 quart glass casserole and microwave for 2 ½ minutes or until soft.

Add the melted butter and the rest of ingredients, except for the toasted sesame seeds.

Beat ingredients together with electric mixer until fluffy then cover with plastic wrap and place in refrigerator for 1 to 2 hours.

Divide the mixture in half using waxed paper and shape into 6 inch logs. Roll logs in sesame seeds. Wrap each log individually and refrigerate or freeze up to one month.

To serve:
Unwrap log and place it on a plate. Microwave the log on low power for 2 to 4 minutes. Remove the log from the microwave and allow to rest for 10 to 15 minutes. Serve with crackers.

Pesto Pate
We make pesto when fresh basil is in season. This recipe is made quickly with a food processor. It is a wonderful way to extend a good thing.

> 8 ounces cream cheese
> 1 cup walnuts
> ½ cup prepared pesto
> ♦ Salt

Use a blender or a food processor to blend the cream cheese, walnuts, pesto and salt. Place the mixture in a serving dish and refrigerate for 3 hours. Serve as a spread with crackers or bread sticks.

Shrimp Toast
I think this recipe was an adaptation of a Chinese dish I have been making for 45 years. **There are 2 ways to cook these, the old and the new:**

For the last 20 years I have used this NEW, healthier method.

Ingredients:
1 pound raw shrimp, peeled, deveined and finely chopped
3 tablespoons green onions, finely diced
1-5 ounce can of water chestnuts, drained and chopped
½ teaspoon salt
¼ teaspoon garlic salt
¼ teaspoon pepper
1 egg white
1½ teaspoons lemon juice
12 thin slices white sandwich bread or thinly sliced baguette

Directions:
Put bread slices under the broiler until toasted brown on one side. Turn bread slices over. Spread un-toasted side with shrimp mixture. Brush with butter. Broil 2 to 3 minutes and serve immediately.
For the sake of posterity, this is the OLD method: It is hard to beat.
Use sandwich bread, cut off crusts, spread with shrimp mixture.
Place shrimp side down in hot oil. Fry until shrimp is done about 2 minutes.
Drain and cut diagonally in quarters.

Rolled Spiced Beef with Lime Peanut Sauce
This is another recipe from Food Day. It comes from a local caterer, Salvador Molly's. Food Day recommended this appetizer recipe because not only are the beef roll ups delicious, they can be made ahead, frozen and popped in the oven when guests arrive. This recipe makes 24 appetizers.

Beef Bundles:

2 pounds sirloin or flank steak, trimmed
1 cup soy sauce
¼ cup dark brown sugar

1 tablespoon sambal oelik chili paste
24 - 1½ by ¼ by ¼ inch pieces of pepper jack cheese, about 8 ozs.
◆ All purpose flour (to coat the cheese pieces)
6 green onions, tops and roots trimmed, cut into 2 inch pieces
3 bell peppers, assorted colors, seeded, trimmed and sliced into ¼ by 2 inch strips
Round wooden toothpicks

Lime Peanut Sauce:

½ cup peanut butter
½ teaspoon minced fresh ginger
½ teaspoon minced roasted garlic
2 tablespoons soy sauce
1½ teaspoon white vinegar
1½ teaspoon fresh lime juice
¾ teaspoon dark sesame oil
2 tablespoon brown sugar
2 tablespoons sambal oelik chili paste
6 tablespoons warm water

Note: The chili paste can be purchased at an Oriental grocery store.

Lime Peanut Sauce:
Combine all ingredients except water in a large bowl. Whisk in water until mixture is smooth. Place sauce in a covered storage container and refrigerate until ready to use. Makes 1 ¼ cups.

To Make Beef Bundles:
Thinly slice meat against the grain on a 45° angle to make pieces 8 inches long. Cut strips in half crosswise to make 4 inch strips. Combine soy sauce, sugar and chili paste together in a shallow bowl.

Stir until the sugar dissolves. Place meat strips in soy mixture and marinate for 20 minutes.

Place cheese in a small bowl, sprinkle with flour to coat evenly. Remove one slice of beef and place it on a clean work surface. At the end of the beef strip closest to you, place a few green onion pieces, one strip of pepper and one piece of cheese. Enclose the vegetables and cheese by rolling the beef up and over the other ingredients. Secure the bundle with a toothpick. Repeat with remaining beef, vegetables and cheese.

After the bundles are completed, place on a lightly oiled cooking sheet. Freeze them uncovered on the baking sheet to set the cheese for baking. Once the bundles are frozen, they can be left on the baking sheet (for ease of cooking) or place them in a freezer storage bag for future use. To cook, place the beef bundles on a baking sheet and bake in a pre-heated 400° oven for 10 to 15 minutes or until the beef is sizzling and the cheese begins to melt. Serve with lime peanut sauce.

Add your favorite appetizer recipes here.

11. SALADS

We didn't have salad every night, but we had it pretty often. Salad was either a scoop of cottage cheese, Mom liked that, or lettuce salad. Lettuce salad referred to ice berg lettuce, rinsed in cold water, drained, and cut into wedges. The wedges were covered with homemade 'French' dressing. It was the dressing that gave all the flavor to the salad. When I was trying to reconstruct this recipe, my brother Larry told me that the recipe included sugar. Larry was right. This recipe for French dressing is from Mom's cookbook. It has Larry's name on it. *I am not making this up:*

French Dressing – Larry

1 cup vegetable oil	1 tablespoons grated onion
½ cup vinegar	1 teaspoon salt
½ cup catsup	2 teaspoons paprika
1 tablespoon lemon juice	¾ cup sugar, (scant)

Blend all ingredients in blender, adding sugar last. Refrigerate. Very Good!

Mom would pour this salad dressing into a glass jar with a screw-on lid and keep it in the refrigerator. It lasted a long time. Whenever we wanted a salad, all Mom had to do was cut up some lettuce, shake the dressing and pour. This was quite the popular salad. The salad is still served in restaurants throughout the Midwest. The last time I was in Illinois I ordered a dinner salad and I got Mom's salad. In addition to the lettuce salad, there was fruit salad.

When I was growing up, every housewife in Waukegan made this dessert fruit salad. There was always at least one version of it at every church pot luck.

Dessert Fruit Salad:

> 1 large can of fruit cocktail, drained
> 1 or 2 fresh bananas
> some grapes, if available
> ½ pint whipping cream, whipped and sweetened
> 1 small package miniature marshmallows

Directions:
Add whipped cream to fruit. Stir in marshmallows. Serve

We also had molded salads that always began with Jello. Plain jello was only served to kids who'd had their tonsels removed and post-operative patients in the hospitals. Jello salads were filled with canned fruit, and fresh bananas. Truly festive jello salads often had miniature marshmallows. This is a jello salad recipe from Mother's cookbook:

Orange Fluff Salad

1 sm.pk. Orange Jell-O®	1 T. sugar
1 cup hot water	1/3 C light cream
½ cup orange juice	1 #2 can of crushed pineapple
2 teaspoon grated orange rind	

Dissolve orange Jell-O® in hot water. Add orange juice, rind, and sugar. When mixture begins to congeal, whip thoroughly. Fold in cream. Add pineapple. Pour into mold to chill.

In the 1970's, my sister Kathy introduced Mom to a special dessert salad made with cranberries, whipped cream, cream cheese, sugar and walnuts. Mom loved this rich, colorful salad and made it for all the major holidays. If Mom was joining us for Christmas dinner, this is what she would be bring. She prepared the salad the day before, and placed it in the freezer. Usually Mom served it at the end of the meal, along with the pies and other desserts. This is good, but it is very, very rich. When served in conjunction with a heavy meal, even a very thin slice is more than enough.

This is the recipe:

Christmas Frozen Salad – Kathy

> 1 can whole berry cranberry sauce
> 2 tablespoons lemon juice
> 8 ounces cream cheese
> ¼ cup mayonnaise
> ¼ cup sifted powdered sugar
> 1 cup walnuts, chopped
> 1 pint whipping cream, whipped

Put cranberries in a bowl and crunch with a fork. Add the lemon juice and stir to blend. Put mixture in a green Tupperware® mold and set aside.

Put cream cheese, mayonnaise, and powdered sugar in a bowl. Use Mixmaster to beat this up and then stir in chopped nuts and fold in the whipped cream. Layer this mixture on top the cranberry mixture (in the Tupperware mold) and put in the freezer until firm.

To serve:
Run hot water over bottom of mold to loosen. Invert on a bed of lettuce.

Today we have many salad choices and these are my favorites. Salads are divided into three categories: vegetable, pasta, meat or fish.

Vegetable Salads

Layered Cobb Salad
This recipe is simple and as good or better than any layered salad I have tried. I've had this recipe a long time and I don't remember where it came from. I would use water chestnuts instead of celery, or half water chestnuts and half celery. This salad will serve at least 10 people. Sharon made this salad for our recent Birthday party.

Salad:
½ head iceberg lettuce
½ pound fresh spinach
4 hard cooked eggs
1 bunch green onions - sliced
3 cups diced chicken breasts

12 slices bacon, crumbled
6 ounces blue cheese - crumbled
2 cups celery - diced

Dressing:
1½ cup sour cream
1½ cup mayonnaise
2 teaspoons cider vinegar
½ teaspoon dried dill weed
1 cup freshly grated parmesan cheese

Directions:
Use a straight sided clear glass bowl. Layer ½ of each the listed salad ingredients in the order given. Make sure the spinach and lettuce has been cut or torn into bite-sized pieces.

Combine ingredients for dressing in a small bowl. Frost salad with ½ the dressing.

Repeat the second layer in the order the ingredients are listed and frost with the balance of the dressing. Sprinkle with 1 cup fresh grated Swiss or parmesan cheese on top of the salad. Cover and refrigerate overnight.

Two-Bean and Corn Salad

This is a wonderful salad for a summer picnic because there is no lettuce to wilt and it actually gets better the longer it sits.

1/3 cup olive oil
2 tablespoons Balsamic vinegar
1 teaspoon ground cumin
1-15 ½ oz can Great Northern beans – drain and rinse beans
1-15 ½ oz can black beans - drain and rinse beans
2 cups frozen corn, thawed
1 medium sized red pepper, chopped
2 small jalapeno peppers, seeded and chopped
1 small red onion, chopped
½ cup cilantro or fresh parsley

Directions:

Whisk oil, vinegar and cumin in bowl to blend. Add the remaining ingredients and toss to coat. Season salad with salt and pepper to taste. Let salad stand for at least 1 hour or up to 4 hours. Toss occasionally.

Ron Yasenchak's *FAMOUS* Hot Corn Salad

My husband created this salad. It is better than good.

Salad: **Dressing:**
4 ears fresh corn,
barely cooked and stripped   ½ cup mayonnaise

3 hard boiled eggs, chopped
1 cup celery, chopped
2 green onions, chopped

4 tablespoons green and red peppers,chopped
2 tablespoons chopped fresh parsley
♦ salt and pepper to taste

1 teaspoon Dijon mustard
1 tablespoon Worcestershire sauce
1 tablespoon white vinegar

2 tablespoons hot sauce

1 teaspoon Tabasco® sauce

Combine salad and dressing. Let set overnight in refrigerator.

Black Bean and Fresh Tomato Salad – Nancy Laws

Nancy made this for a summer bonsai potluck. It may be my favorite salad, and it actually tastes better the next day.

2½ to 3 cups canned black beans, rinsed and drained
1 red bell pepper, seeded and diced
3 green onions, sliced
2 or more ripe plum tomatoes, seeded and sliced
6 tablespoons olive oil
3 tablespoons lemon juice or rice wine vinegar
5 tablespoons chopped cilantro
1 teaspoon freshly ground black pepper
¾ teaspoon salt- if desired
Combine all ingredients and toss gently and serve.

Marinated Mixed Vegetable Salad

I like to serve this in the summer when local produce is at its peak. I don't have a set recipe. The salad ingredients are dependent on availability and my energy level. Some of the vegetables, like pea pods, green onions, sweet red peppers and zucchini are simply cleaned and cut. The potatoes are steamed until just tender but the carrot, asparagus and the broccoli are barely cooked and then immediately cooled. I combine all vegetables with light vinaigrette and refrigerate for at least an hour and up to 8 hours. I usually add some fresh parsley or cilantro and just before serving.

Broiled Romaine Salad

Lee Cheatle is a friend of ours through Bonsai and a professional chef. On the annual Bonsai fishing trip, Lee does most of the cooking. This year, he created a broiled salad. Ron loved the salad, but couldn't remember exactly what was in it or how it was assembled. This version is the salad that Ron re-created, **it serves 4***:*

> 2 tablespoons balsamic vinegar
> 1 dash sugar
> 2 tablespoons olive oil – divided
> 4 ounces prosciutto ham – diced
> 8 large inside leaves of romaine lettuce
> ½ cup crumbled blue or feta cheese

Combine the vinegar and sugar in a small saucepan. Bring the mixture to a boil then reduce the heat and simmer for about 10 minutes or until the mixture is reduced by half and has a thick, syrupy texture. Add the olive oil to the mixture and set aside. Heat the prosciutto in a small sauté pan to brown it and release some of the fat. Place the romaine leaves on a baking sheet, fanning each leaf out. Divide the prosciutto between the leaves and drizzle each leaf with the vinegar mixture. Top with crumbled cheese and place the pan under the broiler. Broil 4 to 6 minutes or until the leaves have wilted and the cheese is melted.

Meat and Fish Salads

The only fish salad I can remember when I was growing up was tuna fish. A can of oil packed tuna was drained and then mixed with Miracle Whip® and a little pickle relish. Today we have fresh and frozen tuna, but there are a lots more choices.

Asparagus/Shrimp Salad – Try this. You'll like it!

I have never measured any of these ingredients so all "measures" are a SWAG. I don't know where I got this recipe. I have made it for so many people I think the recipe is now mine.

Salad:

>1 to 2 pounds fresh asparagus cleaned, cut in 3 inch spears cooked until barely tender crisp and plunged into ice water
>1 head (or less) red or green lettuce, torn into bite sized pieces
>♦ salt, pepper, parsley to taste

Vinegrette Dressing:

>3 hard boiled eggs
>1 small bunch green onions, chopped
>½ to 1 pound salad shrimp, chopped
>½ cup vegetable oil
>2 or 3 tablespoons rice wine vinegar mixed with a little sugar to soften the taste
>1 large clove garlic, finely chopped

Combine oil, vinegar, garlic and spices. Add chopped egg, shrimp and green onions to the salad dressing. Stir to combine all ingredients.

To Serve:
Line a large platter with the lettuce. Arrange cold asparagus on top the lettuce.
Cover the asparagus with the salad dressing.

Fresh Crab Salad – Crab Louie
This is just as easy as shrimp salad, but it is a lot more expensive unless you either catch your own crab or some generous crabber gives you one from his catch. If you have to buy crab I would at least consider purchasing fresh crab meat at a fish market.

The true cost is about the same as buying the whole crab, cracking and cleaning it.

Fresh crabmeat is served with an assortment of salad greens. The salad is garnished with slices of black olives and hard boiled eggs. I serve it with a Thousand Island dressing.

Warm Chicken Salad
This is a great summer salad. I can't eat pineapple anymore, so I use fresh pears or fresh peaches. This salad is always a hit.

        1 to 2 tablespoons olive oil
        1 whole chicken breast, skinned, boned
        and sliced into ½ inch strips
        1 red bell pepper, sliced into thin strips
        1 green bell pepper, sliced into thin strips
        1 small bunch of green onions, sliced
        1 small can sliced water chestnuts
        1 red onion, thinly sliced
        1 teaspoon vinegar
        1 teaspoon Worcestershire sauce
        1 fresh pineapple, cut into small chunks

(or mango, papaya, or peaches)
½ cup walnuts, chopped coarsely
1 head romaine lettuce or mixture of salad greens cleaned and torn into bite sized pieces.

Place one tablespoon olive oil in a heavy bottomed non-stick sauté pan or a cast iron skillet. Heat oil to medium high and add chicken pieces. Stir-fry, quickly browning an all sides, 2 to 3 minutes. Add the vegetables, salt and pepper. Stir in the vinegar and Worcestershire sauce. When the chicken is cooked through, add the pineapple and walnuts. Remove the pan from the heat. Pour the chicken mixture over prepared lettuce. Toss and serve with crusty French bread.

Add your favorite salad recipes here.

12. SOUPS

SOUP'S ON!!

At one time this was a familiar phrase. It was never used at my house because we never had soup. That's not quite true, there was soup at my house, and it came out of a can.

Mom used canned cream of chicken and cream of mushroom soups to cook tuna noodle casserole and her famous pork chops and rice. We never had home made soup, ever. She kept a couple of cans of chicken noodle soup on hand in case someone got sick.

My mother didn't like soup and didn't want anything to do with it. As for Dad, he wanted real food. I remember eating Campbell's chicken noodle soup for lunch. I still like it and I keep a stash of canned soup in my cupboard for times when I feel punk. I think of soups and casseroles as part of the same chapter. I suppose that is why I combined them here.

Note: Punk is an old, old term, probably from my Grandpa's logging camps. It means not sick enough to miss school or church or work; not well enough to enjoy a full meal. This recipe for turkey soup is from my mother's cookbook. Mom never made anything like this while we were growing up. Perhaps after all the kids moved away, she actually had some turkey left from a huge bird. I know that if she made this recipe she would have followed it to the letter.

Old Fashioned Turkey Soup

Ingredients:

3 quarts water
1 tablespoon salt
1 bay leaf
1 tablespoon Worcestershire sauce

2 cups sliced carrots
1 cup diced turnips
2 cups chopped celery

1 left-over turkey carcass
¼ cup chopped parsley
♦ Salt and pepper to taste

2 cups chopped
potatoes

Directions:

Use a large stockpot. Heat water, combine turkey carcass with water, bay leaf and Worcestershire sauce. Bring to a boil, reduce heat and simmer 1½ hours. Remove carcass, pull off any meat remaining on bones and discard the carcass. Return meat to the stockpot. Add celery, onions, carrots and turnips. Cover and simmer, covered for 30 minutes. Add potatoes. Simmer, covered for 30 minutes. Stir in parsley. Season to taste.

There are few meals I like better than home-made soup. I make oyster stew, clam chowder, fish stew, black bean, navy bean, pea, squash and lentil soup. I also boil chicken and turkey carcasses and use the broth for cooking. As much as I like it, I don't make soup all that often because Ron is only luke warm on soup, especially my home- made soup. For example, I make black bean soup when I have a meaty ham bone.

- Ron agrees that it tastes good, but it looks like dark, rich, lumpy mud. It is very hard for him to get excited over flavorful mud.

- Navy bean soup looks better, but he thinks it smells like wallpaper paste and it generates absolute gas wars that no one wins.
- If I boil up a turkey carcass, add some vegetables and rice and try to pass it off as soup, he just rolls his eyes.
- But if I make good oyster stew, he vows he would marry me again.
- Finally, when I make Bouillabaisse or creamy clam chowder, he gets positively sappy.

Sharon makes wonderful soup and the best pea soup, ever. She ensures the flavor and quality of her soup by buying a meaty ham bone from Honey Baked Ham®. *She also follows recipes.*

This is a recipe from Sunset's Seafood Cookbook©, 1967 edition Seafood Bisque:

This original recipe served 16. I modified the recipe to serve 4. It is very, very rich and very, very good. Be gracious with the compliments you will surely receive.

Ingredients:

1/3 cup butter (divided)
¼ cup instant type all purpose flour
1 – 7 ½ ounce can of minced clams
2 cups. milk
2 cups whipping cream
2 green onions, diced
½ pound cooked Dungeness crab meat
¼ pound cooked salad shrimp
¼ cup dry white wine
1½ tablespoons dry sherry

Directions:

Chop green onions and set aside.

Melt 3 tablespoons of butter in a heavy bottomed pan. Blend in flour and cook 2 minutes, do not allow flour to brown. Drain liquid from clams, and stir in liquid. (reserve clams)

Slowly stir in the milk and light cream. Cook until mixture thickens. In a sauté pan, melt remaining 2 ½ tablespoons butter and sauté onions until limp. Add crab, shrimp, and drained clams. Continue to sauté over medium heat until seafood is hot.

Add the saute'd seafood, onion mixture to the soup. Stir in white wine and sherry.

Ginger Scented Butternut Squash Soup
This recipe calls for frozen butternut squash.

*Hint: **Fresh always trumps frozen anything.** I'd wait until autumn to make this soup, and I'd use **fresh delicata squash.** **Note:** Frozen squash would save time and energy and it would certainly expand the window of opportunity for this hearty soup.*

Ingredients:
3 cups low sodium chicken broth
2 - 10 ounce packages of frozen cooked butternut squash
1 cup unsweetened apple sauce
♦ about 1 teaspoon of salt or to taste
1 teaspoon ground ginger, or more
½ cup whipping cream

Directions:
- Combine frozen squash with chicken broth in a medium sized pot over medium heat.
- Cook, spooning the broth over the squash until squash has defrosted, 12 minutes.
- Add apple sauce, salt, sugar and ginger, whisk to combine.
- Increase the heat, bringing mixture to a boil.
- Reduce heat to medium low, add cream, simmer gently for 30 minutes.

Fish Soups

Cioppino or bouillabaisse are both tomato based soups featuring shellfish. Cioppino is Portuguese; Bouillabaisse is French. There are dozens of recipes for both of these soups. They are all as good as the shellfish and regular fish that died for the cause. This is my recipe. I started making it whenever we spent a weekend at the beach in a room that had a kitchen.

My version includes some short cuts, but it always tastes good.

- Saute Vegetables: Carrots, onions, garlic, mushrooms, are all cleaned and sliced, seasoned and sautéed in olive oil.
- Herbs and spices: I use parsley, paprika, and thyme plus salt and pepper.
- Tomatoes: I use a large jar of marinara sauce…some are better than others, most are pretty good.
- Additional liquid: I use the marinara jar as my measurer, and I don't rinse it out before adding the wine and water. Fill one third of the jar with decent red wine. Top the jar off with water.
- **Shellfish: I buy whatever is fresh and available:** Dungeness crab, shrimp, manila clams, scallops, mussels, etc.
- Fish: I also like to add a little white fish for the change in variety and texture. Halibut is always good; salmon just gets lost.

To assemble:

Sauté vegetables until tender, add large jar of marina sauce. Add wine. Let flavors meld.

Add water, adjust seasonings, add shellfish and white fish. Cover and cook until fish is done, clams are open, shellfish is heated through. It doesn't take long, 5 or 6 minutes.

Serve with large bibs, and plenty of crusty French bread, and a lovely bottle of Oregon Pinot Noir.

Pot Sticker Chicken Soup

I made this, but with home made stock. It could not be any easier and it is very good.

Ingredients:
2 - 14 ounce cans reduced sodium fat free chicken broth
or one 32 ounce box
2 cloves garlic, minced
1 fresh green or red jalapeño chili, seeded and mixed –
(this is the secret ingredient!)
16 to 18 frozen pot stickers
1 ½ cups spinach (or ¼ of a 10 ounce box of frozen spinach,
thawed, drained and squeezed to release extra moisture, or
my new favorite, **kale!**
Hot chili oil (optional)

Directions:
Simmer chicken broth with jalapeño chili for about 5 minutes. Add
frozen pot stickers and simmer for an additional 5 minutes. Add
spinach or kale and simmer until the spinach is just wilted, but still
green. Serve.

Add your favorite soup recipes here.

13. SAUCES

At our house, Ron is the king of sauces. He <u>always </u>follows the recipe; never gets distracted; and does a wonderful job, first time, every time. He dirties every pot in the kitchen and is completely unapologetic. Ron has made all of these sauces. Most of them are loaded with fat. All of them taste great and enhance the main ingredient.

Sauces for Beef

Chanterelle Mushroom Sauce
Ron modified this recipe. He decreased the stock to ½ cup and added ½ cup heavy cream.

Ingredients:
8 ozs. fresh chanterelle mushrooms, sliced
¼ cup butter
roasting pan juices
1 to 1¾ C Pinot Noir wine

1 cup beef stock - If you don't have home made beef stock, use canned, low-sodium beef or chicken stock.

Directions:
♦ Saute the chanterelles in ¼ cup melted butter until they are soft and have released most of their moisture.
♦ Deglaze the pan used to cook the meat with wine. Pour the wine and pan juices into the chanterelle mixture.
♦ Add beef broth and heavy cream. Bring up to temperature.
♦ Serve the sauce with the meat.

Port Wine and Mushroom Sauce

This mushroom sauce is quicker, easier and lower in fat than the previous one.

Ingredients:
1 tablespoon flour
black pepper
1½ cup sliced shitake, cremini
or other fresh wild mushrooms
¾ cup beef broth or stock, (divided)
1 shallot, finely chopped
2 tablespoons tomato paste
1 tablespoon Worchester sauce, (W. sauce)
1/3 cup port wine
1 tablespoon red wine vinegar

Directions:
Measure flour into a plastic bag, add pepper and mushrooms, toss and set aside.
Use a small skillet. Heat 2 tablespoons broth, add shallots, cook until soft. Add tomato paste, and W.sauce. Cook 1 to 2 minutes. Add the remaining broth and vinegar. Bring to a boil. Add mushroom mixture. Cook until mushrooms are soft.

Sauces for Pork:

Port Wine Sauce

3 cups beef stock (use *unsalted,*
home-made beef or chicken stock)
1 cup port wine
2 tablespoons butter
½ cup green onions, diced

1 cup sliced mushrooms

Combine stock and port wine. Simmer until reduced to 1 cup. (about 1 hour). When pork is done and very tender, remove from pan and set aside. Push drippings off to one side, and use the roasting pan to finish this sauce. Melt the butter, add onions and mushrooms. Sauté incorporating the pan drippings. Finish the sauce by adding the port wine reduction

To Serve:
Slice pork. Serve with sauce over the pork or on the side.

Apple Cider Pork Tenderloin Sauce

The pork tenderloin has been seasoned, browned, and roasted in a 425°oven for 15 minutes. It has been removed from the skillet, covered with foil and will rest for about 15 minutes while the sauce is being prepared.
Combine pan drippings with two 2 teaspoons butter
Add two Granny Smith apples, that have been peeled, cored and sliced into 16 wedges. Sauté until lightly browned, 5 to 7 minutes. Transfer the apples to a serving platter.
Add one cup of low sodium fat-free chicken broth and 2/3 cup apple cider.
Dissolve ½ teaspoon cornstarch in 1 tablespoon water. Add the cornstarch mixture to the sauce and boil until thickened and reduced to about 1 cup. Stir in 2 tablespoons of cider vinegar, and any juices that accumulated on the platter.

Sauces for Fish

Cool as a Cucumber Sauce
This sauce can be used with crab cakes, scallops, halibut, grilled chicken, pork or steamed spiced shrimp.

1- 10 ounce cucumber, peeled, seeded and coarsely shredded
¾ cup plain yogurt
2 tablespoons minced fresh dill
2 tablespoons green onions or ¼ cup minced fresh chives
¼ teaspoon kosher salt
½ teaspoon freshly ground pepper
- Pinch of cayenne

Squeeze shredded cucumber to remove fluid, leaving about 2/3 cup cucumber. Stir cucumber, yogurt, dill, green onions, salt, pepper and cayenne together. Chill, taste and adjust seasonings.

Curried Yogurt Sauce
Use this sauce with halibut, sea bass, grouper or grilled chicken. It can also be used as a base for curried chicken or seafood salad.

Ingredients:
¼ teaspoon minced fresh ginger root
¼ teaspoon minced garlic
¼ teaspoon dry mustard
½ teaspoon kosher salt
1 teaspoon curry powder
¼ teaspoon paprika
½ teaspoon coriander
1 teaspoon vegetable oil
6 Tablespoon plain yogurt

Directions:
Mash ginger, garlic, mustard and salt to form a paste. Set aside.
Mix curry, paprika and coriander in a small bowl. Set aside.

Use a small skillet to heat oil, add garlic paste. Sauté for one minute. Sprinkle the combined spices over the paste. Sauté for 1 minute…don't let it burn.

Scrape mixture into a small bowl. Stir in 1 teaspoon of yogurt to make a paste. Gradually mix in the remaining yogurt. Chill. Taste and adjust seasonings.

Sauce Verde:

> 1 cup mayonnaise
> ¼ cup honey
> 3¾ teaspoons of prepared mustard
> 1 tablespoon fresh cilantro leaves, minced
> ¼ cup fresh parsley, finely minced
> 1¼ teaspoon minced fresh chives

Directions:
Combine all the ingredients listed above and refrigerate for at least 2 hours for flavors to fully develop. Served the sauce chilled for dipping the smoked salmon.

Easier Sauces, Becky's Specialties

Aiole Sauce
This simple mayonnaise recipe is from the Wildwood Restaurant in Portland.

> ¼ cup mayonnaise
> 2 tablespoons milk
> 1 tablespoon fresh lemon juice
> 1 clove garlic, minced
> Blend all ingredients together, set aside.

Blender Hollandaise Sauce

> 3 egg yolks
> 2 tablespoon lemon juice
> ¼ teaspoon salt
> ½ cup butter
> • pinch of cayenne

Directions:
Have egg yolks, lemon juice, cayenne and salt ready in the blender.
Heat butter to bubbling stage, do not brown
Cover blender and process on high.
After 3 seconds, while still processing, add butter in a steady stream.
Serve at once.

Secrets to Great, Fast, and EASY sauces:

If you are trying to impress some special someone with your cooking skill. By all means add a fancy sauce to your main dish. If you can convince Mr. Ron to help you, you'll have a great sauce. However you'll have to put up with him in your kitchen and he *will* take full credit for his masterpiece.

There is another option: Knorr® makes several pre-packaged sauce mixes. That are all fast and easy. My personal favorites are Hollindaise, Bearnaise and green Peppercorn Sauce. If you choose this option be sure to do these two things:

1. Don't cheat on the ingredients. If the mix calls for butter, use butter, not margerine. If it calls for sour cream, use sour cream. Never use fake sour cream.

2. Get rid of the empty package before your guests arrive. There is no need for anyone to know you occasionally get a little help.

Tips to save a sauce in trouble:

Some times things go sideways. If your sauce is too thin, or lumpy, ad this magic smoother-outer:

½ tablespoon room temperature butter
½ tablespoon flour
½ tablespoon parmesan cheese

Mix these ingredients together to form a paste. Add about ¼ teasoon of magic at a time to the problem sauce until the rescue is complete.

Lemon Caper Sauce

2 tablespoons fresh lemon juice
2 tablespoons minced red onion or shallots
2 tablespoons olive oil
1 tablespoon drained capers, chopped
1 teaspoon chopped fresh thyme
½ teaspoon grated lemon peel

Whisk above ingredients together, season with salt and pepper and serve with broiled or baked salmon.

Tarragon Butter Sauce
Place following ingredients in a sauce pan and bring to a boil:

¼ cup dry white wine
the juice from 1 lemon

8 tablespoons unsalted butter, cut into ½ inch cubes
2 teaspoons chopped fresh tarragon leaves

Add your favorite sauce recipes here…

14. POTATOES and/or RICE

In Waukegan, if we were out of potatoes, we had no food. Potatoes were cheap. How cheap were they? They were so cheap that we had potatoes every day for dinner and lots of times for breakfast as well. Perhaps you have heard or read about a peck of potatoes, or potato sacks.

When I was growing up in the 1950's, a person could buy a 50-pound sack of potatoes. Mostly, the people who bought potatoes by the sack either owned a restaurant, or had a really large family, or were very thrifty. Dad was on the cheap side of thrifty and he loved potatoes. We always bought potatoes by the fifty pound sack.

We ate potatoes every night with supper. They were prepared in the following ways:

- **Mashed Potatoes** were peeled and then boiled until fork tender or until the water boiled off. If any water remained, it was discarded. The potatoes were mashed in the pan with a little milk, some salt and a generous pat of margarine.
- **Roasted Potatoes** were peeled, quartered, and cooked with a Pot Roast:
- **Boiled with Cabbage and Ham** See Pork section
- **Baked potatoes** were always wrapped in foil.
- **French Fried:** Sometime during the 1950's we bought a French Fry cooker for the express purpose of creating French fries at home. They were more work than you would think: I remember peeling and cutting potatoes and then soaking the cut potatoes in ice water. I can't remember if they were worth all the trouble.
- **Potato Salad** was made for picnics and church suppers. Potatoes were peeled, boiled, chilled, diced and then mixed with chopped hard boiled eggs, pickle relish, chopped onions and

chopped celery. All ingredients were bound together with a generous dollop of Miracle Whip®.

- **Fried If we had left over boiled potatoes, (a rare event)** they would be chopped and fried in bacon grease for breakfast.
- **Sweet potatoes were served once a year, with Thanksgiving dinner.** They were peeled, boiled, cooled, and either sliced or cut into chunks. When the turkey was done (and the oven was available) the sweet potatoes were placed in an oven-proof bowl, topped with margarine, brown sugar, and tiny marshmallows.

Fast forward sixty years:

Mashed potatoes couldn't be any easier. I buy them frozen or in a free-dried pouch.

Baked potatoes take 2 to 3 minutes to bake in the microwave. I usually start them in the microwave and finish them in the oven.

Sweet potatoes are available year-round. Our friend Jan Kent introduced Ron and me to baked sweet potatoes. They are great, but the skins tend to split and sweet, sticky potato will oozes out and burns if they stay in the oven too long.

French fries are a restaurant standby that I avoid as much as possible.

Potato salad rarely appears at our house. I really enjoyed mom's version and any thing else just didn't cut it. I can't replicate mom's recipe because I would have to buy Miracle Whip®.

Rice: We rarely had rice. Mom used Uncle Ben's Converted Rice® for her signature pork dish. And we always had a box of minute rice, just in case we got invited to a wedding. I don't believe we ever had rice as a side dish unless you consider Spanish rice. ***See American Food, page 7 for this Butrick Street regular.***

I prepare potatoes pretty often. It is possible that old habits die hard. However, I don't go to this much trouble for mashed potatoes. Instead, I buy either frozen or dried potato flakes in a box. They're not great, but they're not awful, either. Occasionally we have garlic mashed potatoes. I peel, quarter, and boil Yukon gold potatoes until they are barely done. I use a separate sauce pan to simmer chopped garlic in about ½ cup of light cream and a little butter. The potatoes are drained and riced; the garlic cream mixture is added, along with salt and pepper.

We also have rice, risotto, and quite a bit of pasta. I am trying to convince Ron that Couscous and quinoa are good things, but it is a hard sell.

Gratineed Gold Potatoes
This is a Food Day recipe. I made this dish one night for Dave and Gabrielle. David liked it so much, he typed out the recipe for me. My children have learned that if I come up with a winner, it is a good idea to get it in writing.

> ¾ pound Yukon Gold or other yellow potatoes
> Salt and freshly ground black pepper
> 2 tablespoons grated parmesan cheese

Directions:
Preheat broiler. Wash potatoes and cut into ¼-inch slices. Place in steamer basket over water, cover with a lid and bring the water to a boil. Steam for 15 minutes. Place in an oven-proof pie plate or lasagna pan. Sprinkle with salt and pepper to taste and with cheese. Place under broiler for 2 minutes or until cheese melts. Serve and enjoy.

Gabrielle's Holiday Mashed Potatoes:
Gabrielle surprised us one Thanksgiving with a special potato dish. She peeled white potatoes and sweet potatoes and cooked them separately. The cooked potatoes were cooled, peeled, combined and then mashed. She added at least 8 ounces of cream cheese and at least one full cube of butter along with some salt and pepper. The potato mixture was scooped into an oven proof dish and baked in the oven at 350° while the turkey was done and 'resting.' Gabrielle made roughly 6 or 8 pounds of potatoes and they all disappeared.

Baked Potato Skins
Ron never eats the skin from his baked potato. I think it is the best part. About 10 years ago 'Baked Potato Skins' started turning up as an appetizer at local restaurants. I don't make these very often, but they are good. There is no specific recipe that I use, so there are no specific ingredients or amounts. This is a general guideline for how I prepare potato skins:

To prepare potatoes:
Bake a bunch of potatoes, 6 – 8 at 400° for an hour or until they are done. Let the potatoes cool completely. Cut each potato in half and scoop out potato, leaving the skin intact if possible. Save the scooped out potato to be used for something else. (See Renaissance Meals, Chapter 9). Fill the potato skin halves with something you like. I use crisp bacon, chopped green onions, sliced black olives and chopped red pepper. Cover the filling with shredded sharp cheddar cheese.
Place the filled potato skins on a baking sheet. Bake at 350° for 15 minutes.
Serve with sour cream. Even Ron loves these.

Hasselback Potatoes

This is an easy Scandinavian recipe. The potatoes look good and taste great.

Ingredients:

4 medium sized Yukon Gold potatoes (peeled and cut in half lengthwise)

½ cup white bread crumbs or Panko

½ cup fresh parmesan cheese, grated

1 tablespoon olive oil or melted butter - plus

2 – 3 tablespoon olive oil to drizzle over potatoes

1 teaspoon sweet paprika

- salt to taste

Directions:

- Preheat oven to 450°. Oil a large glass baking dish.
- Prepare the peeled, halved potatoes, placing each half, cut side down, on a cutting board. Arrange 2 chop sticks one on each side of the potato and slice thinly across.
- *The chopsticks keep you from cutting through the potato.*
- Process bread crumbs, cheese, oil and seasonings in a food processor. Transfer mixture to a shallow dish.
- Drizzle potatoes with oil, carefully bend to fan out the slices.
- Roll potato in crumb mixture.
- Arrange potatoes in a baking dish. Cover with foil and bake 30 minutes.
- Remove foil and continue cooking until crumbs are brown and potatoes are cooked, about 10 more minutes.

Baked Sweet Potatoes with Maple – Jalapeño Sour Cream

This recipe is from Cuisine at Home. They suggest this treatment of sweet potatoes as an alternative to traditional sweeter than sweet potatoes. It is very easy. Buy medium sized sweet potatoes and don't cut them.

For the sweet potatoes:

4 sweet potatoes, scrubbed and dried.

Rub with oil, salt and pepper. Bake at 450° for 40 – 45 minutes or until the flesh is soft when pierced.

Sweet Potato Topping:

½ cup sour cream or plain yogurt

1 tablespoon pure maple syrup

2 teaspoons jalapeño pepper, seeded and minced

1 teaspoon fresh lime juice

Combine listed ingredients. Chill until ready to serve with the sweet potatoes.

Rice

Ron and I took a Chinese cooking class years ago. A young man taught the class. He'd learned how to prepare Chinese food from his mother. One of the first things we learned was how to prepare rice.

Like many of my recipes, this one offers broad general guidelines.

1. Purchase long grain rice. The price per pound declines significantly as the quantity increases.
2. Place about a cup of rice in a heavy 1 or 2 quart sauce pan.
3. Fill the pan about half way with cold tap water.
4. Wash the rice by rubbing the individual grains of rice between your fingers.
5. A milky residue will be released. Drain off the water and repeat the washing process 4 or 5 times or until the water is almost clear.

6. Pour tap water over the rice. Allow about an inch of water above the rice.
7. Place pan over medium high heat, uncovered. Heat until water is just starting to boil.
8. Reduce the heat to medium low. Cover the pan and allow to cook for 25 to 30 minutes.
9. Take pan off heat. Leave cover on until ready to serve. Fluff the rice with a fork and serve.
10. This makes more rice than I ever need. I save the left over rice for a different meal on another day. It works well for fried rice, sushi or domburi.

Wild Rice is served with many wild game dishes. It has a slightly different texture and color, it's almost black, so it can be used effectively with white or brown rice. I don't think wild rice is anything to rave about. It's okay. Risotto or Aborio Rice is truly the king of rice.

Raw Aborio rice can be difficult to find and chances are it will be expensive. In general terms, it is first sauted in butter or olive oil and then cooked slowly with chicken stock. It is a hands-on procedure that takes close to an hour. The result is a creamy almost pudding like consistency. It is very good. I have conned Ron into making this for me. I lack the patience to do it myself.

Fortunately for us, there are several prepackaged risottos on the market and everyone that we have tried has been tasty... and easy.

Notes...

15. NON-Meat Meals, Eggs

In Waukegan the very idea of non-meat meals would have been my dad's version of an oxymoron. If 'Pork Fat Ruled', and it absolutely did, the idea of a meal without meat was positively Catholic and simply unacceptable.

Today a large segment of the population has sworn off meat and designated themselves not as super Catholics, but vegetarians, and vegans. Ron and I both like meat but we do enjoy some non-meat meals. Some meals feature eggs. Others rely on cheeses and pasta. Many Oriental dishes feature vegetables with small portions of meat for flavoring. I have included a sampling of each category. There are also a couple of casseroles that are pretty good.

Eggs: At my house on Butrick Street, eggs had three primary uses:

Breakfast: Eggs were fried, over easy, in bacon grease and served with bacon and toast.

Deviled eggs: These mid-western 'Whore De Or vies' followed fried eggs in frequency and popularity. Deviled eggs were a reliable option at each potluck supper.

Baking: Eggs were a key ingredient in home baked cookies and pre-packaged cake mixes.

Trailing far behind in the egg parade, we had the annual recycling of left-over Easter eggs. These colorful remnants were used in egg salad sandwiches and tinted potato salad. The subject of eggs calls for a word or two about breakfast.

Breakfast on Butrick Street:
I remember eating breakfast occasionally but it certainly was not a daily event. During the week we could eat cold cereal, (NOT), or

sleep an additional 5 minutes. On Sunday, there was rarely time for a real breakfast. However, on a few rare occasions Dad would buy a coffee cake and we would eat it before we went to church.

Saturday was a real breakfast day. There wasn't much variety; breakfast was bacon, eggs and toast. Once in a while we would have left over ham with our eggs and every now and then we would have sausage with our eggs. We never had omelets, scrambled or poached eggs. Eggs were fried in our never-ending supply of bacon grease. Just to be safe, mom kept a big can of left-over grease right next to the stove.

When we were short on eggs and long on stale bread, we would have French toast. We never had sweet rolls and, until Larry bought an interest in the <u>Donut Kettle</u>, we never had doughnuts.

My family missed out on some great egg dishes. I have included some good egg recipes and a few tips to help you get started.

Different Ways to Cook Eggs

Omelets: There are a few secrets to a good omelet. An omelet only takes two to three minutes to cook so it is absolutely necessary have everything ready *before* starting.
Pan: Use an 8 or 9 inch Teflon coated sauté pan
Eggs: I use 3 eggs for 2 omelets.
Fillings: A plain or basic omelet isn't filled with anything, ergo plain.
- One step up from a plain omlet is the ever popular cheese omelet: Hard cheeses or semi-hard cheeses like Parmesan, Cheddar or Swiss work very well. Grate or shred the cheese so it will mclt quickly.

- Optional vegetable fillings include raw chopped green onions, black olives, or tomatoes. Sautéed fresh zucchini, mushrooms, or asparagus also work very well.
- For a heartier omelet add meat. You can use bacon (fried until crisp and crumbled into pieces), or use any diced cooked meat. This would include left over steak, ham, or sausage.
- A seafood omelet could include shrimp, crab or any precooked fish.
- Plates: The table should be set with everything but the individual plates. The plates should be stacked and ready for the omelets as they slide out of the sauté pan.

To prepare a perfect omelet:

Break 1 to 2 eggs per omelet into a small bowl. Use the broken egg shell as a measurer and fill the ½ shell with tap water, for each egg) add salt and pepper to taste. Combine the eggs, water and seasonings with a whisk or a fork. Set aside.

Preheat Teflon sauté pan over medium high heat.

Melt ½ teaspoon of butter, tilting the pan to allow butter to foam and cover the bottom and sides. Pour 1 serving of omelet mixture into pan. Cook 1 to 2 minutes to let the mixture set. Shake the pan to help egg mixture cook evenly. When egg mixture has set, but is still runny, add fillings and top with shredded cheese. Continue to cook for a minute or 2 until the omelet is lightly browned and the cheese is mostly melted. Fold the omelet onto the plate. Note: The omlet will continue to cook. Top the omelet with fresh parsley, sour cream, salsa or nothing at all.

Perfect Soft Scrambled Eggs

If you make scrambled eggs with milk, they can get watery. If you just use eggs, they can be dry and tough. If you stir the eggs constantly as they are cooking, they end up looking like lumpy custard. This is my method for soft scrambled eggs. It is easy and just about fool proof.

This recipe serves 2.

½ teaspoon of butter
4 eggs
2 tablespoons of sour cream
- salt and pepper to taste

Crack the eggs into a small bowl and beat lightly with a fork. Add the sour cream, salt and pepper and stir lightly to combine. Preheat a Teflon sauté pan to medium high heat. Add the butter to the pan. It will melt very quickly. Tilt the pan so the butter will cover the bottom and sides of the pan. Cook the eggs stirring gently so they don't get brown or glob together. They will be perfectly cooked soft scrambled eggs in 2 to 3 minutes. If you prefer dryer scrambled eggs, add 1 to 3 minutes to cooking time. When the eggs are done to your standards, remove the pan from heat. Plate the eggs and serve immediately.

Poached Eggs:
Poached eggs are a lower fat alternative to fried or scrambled eggs. They can be a little tricky. There may be a better method, but this works for me.

Bring 2 to 3 inches of water to a simmer in a Teflon sauté pan. Place each egg to be poached in a separate bowl. (I use a custard cup.) Stir the simmering water with a spoon and then gently slide each egg into the water.

Simmer the eggs until the whites and yolks are set. Use a rubber spatula to keep eggs from sticking to the pan and a slotted spoon and slide eggs out and back into the custard cup one at a time.

Perfect Hard Boiled Eggs:
Sometimes it doesn't matter if the hard boiled eggs peel easily or if they are cooked through. Sometimes it does. I found this method years ago. If the eggs are reasonably fresh this method will almost give you hard boiled eggs that peel easily, retain their color and look good enough to slice and put on top anything.

Place fresh cold eggs in a sauce pan, be careful not to crowd the eggs. Fill the sauce pan with enough cold tap water to cover the eggs. Add a pinch of salt to prevent eggs from cracking. Heat sauce pan until water comes to a full, rolling boil. Allow the eggs to boil for 5 minutes. Take the pan off the heat and cover with a lid. Allow the eggs to cool in the water to room temperature. To peel, fracture egg shell into small pieces and peel under water.

Perfect 3 Minute Eggs:
Follow the same directions as those given for hard boil eggs. Instead of allowing the eggs to cool to room temperature, remove them from the water after 4 minutes, place in an egg cup, cut off the top of the shell and serve. I am not sure how or why this works, but this method and 4 minutes of waiting will result in a perfect 3 minute egg.

Deviled Eggs
My grandson, Connor, wouldn't eat deviled eggs if you paid him. However most <u>normal</u> people like them, and the rest of my family loves them. Mom made deviled eggs with Miracle Whip® and pickle relish. She sprinkled paprika on the top. **This is how I make them.**

6 hard cooked eggs, peeled and sliced in half lengthwise
3 tablespoons mayonnaise
1 teaspoon Dijon Mustard
1 teaspoon freshly squeezed lemon juice
½ teaspoon hot pepper sauce
1 tablespoon fresh minced parsley or any other fresh herbs
- salt and freshly ground pepper to taste

Remove yolks and place them in a small bowl with mayonnaise, mustard, lemon juice and hot pepper sauce. Mash the egg mixture until smooth, then stir in herbs and salt and pepper. Stuff equal amounts of the yolk mixture into hollows of egg whites. Refrigerate eggs until ready to serve. Garnish each egg with paprika, a sprig of dill or chopped chives.

Egg Test
If you are not sure if your eggs are fresh put them to this simple test: Place raw eggs in a bowl of water.
- *If the eggs lie on the bottom of the bowl, they are fresh.*
- *If the eggs tilt so the large end is up, they are getting old.*
- *If the eggs float, they are rotten.*

Mystery Eggs
Are they hard boiled of not? This is another test: Place the suspect egg on a countertop. Give the egg a twirl.
- *If the egg spins, it is hard boiled.*
- *If it wobbles, it is fresh.*
- *If it breaks, it's too bad.*

This quiche recipe is from Cindy Compton. If there was ever a contest for 'Real men don't eat quiche, Wylie would win, hands down. We met Wylie in 1970 when Wylie, his wife Marge and their infant son Jeff moved into their house directly across the street from us. David played with Jeff. I shopped, golfed and bowled with Marge. Ron golfed and hunted with Wylie. We all camped together.

Things change. We moved away. Wylie and Marge divorced, Wylie moved to eastern Oregon and the children all grew up. David met Jeff again in high school. Then, one night, Jeff showed up unannounced at our house on Colina Vista Ave. Jeff still had string-straight-white-blond hair, bright blue eyes and a crooked little smile. David asked us if we remembered this kid. Of course we did even though we hadn't seen him for 10 years. A really nice, cute little boy had turned into a grown up version of himself.

David and Jeff arranged for a father/son golf match, and it was a success. After that golf date, Ron made a point of seeing Wylie whenever he traveled to Eastern Oregon. In the summer of 2000, Wylie and Cindy visited us at our A-Frame. That October, we spent a weekend at their vacation home in Black Butte. Cindy made this quiche and Wylie liked it just as much as the rest of us.

Compton Quiche

Ingredients:
10 slices white bread, cubed, and crusts trimmed.
½ pound freshly grated cheese
¾ pound crisp bacon, crumbled. Ham or sausage would also work.
6 eggs
3 cups milk

Line a 9 x 12 pan with bread cubes. Beat eggs and milk together. Add layer of cheese and bacon. Place in the refrigerator overnight. Bake at 350° for about 45 minutes or until hot and bubbly.

Quiche Lorraine
This is so simple and so good. If it wasn't absolutely loaded with fat, it would be perfect.

9 inch unbaked pie shell
½ pound bacon, fried crisp and crumbled
1½ cups freshly grated Swiss cheese
1½ cups light cream
3 eggs
¾ t. salt
- Dash nutmeg, cayenne and black pepper

Sprinkle crumbled bacon on the bottom of the pie shell. Sprinkle grated cheese over the bacon. Beat the eggs with the cream and seasonings and pour mixture over the cheese. Bake in a 375° oven for 35 to 40 minutes. The quiche is done when the top is brown and the center is firm. Cool 10 minutes before serving.

Vesta's Salmon Quiche
This recipe is from the Sequim paper. It is incredibly easy and very good.

Combine following ingredients in a blender:

3 eggs
½ cup butter, melted
¼ teaspoon salt and ¼ teaspoon pepper
3 tablespoons onion, finely chopped
½ cup Bisquick®
1½ cups milk

To assemble the quiche:
Place 1- 16 ounce can of salmon, flaked (or left over baked salmon) and chopped black olives in a 10 inch quiche pan. Pour the egg/milk mixture over salmon. Sprinkle with 1 cup of grated swiss, mozzarella or cheddar cheese. Bake in a preheated 350° oven for 45 minutes.

Remove quiche from the oven. Let it set for 10 minutes before cutting.

Seafood Frittata

A frittata is an open faced Italian omelet. I have ordered frittatas in restaurants. My favorite frittatas include Italian sausage, mushrooms, shallots, sweet peppers, tomatoes and cheese. I haven't really followed the recipe exactly. I did come close substituting one fish for another and the result was A-OK. I use a cast iron skillet and I have everything ready because this goes together very quickly. Caution, if the seafood has been frozen it will need to be drained before adding it to this dish.

Ingredients:
¼ cup clarified butter
1/3 cup sliced mushrooms
¼ cup thinly sliced green onions
½ tablespoon minced fresh garlic
3 eggs
¼ to ½ cup half and half
½ cup salmon cut into 1 inch pieces
½ cup bay or quartered sea scallops
½ cup rock fish cut into 1 inch pieces
½ cup cooked bay shrimp
1 tablespoon fresh lemon juice
2 to 3 tablespoons white wine
1 large whole tomato, sliced

Add clarified butter to the skillet and bring to temperature over medium high heat.
Add mushrooms, onions and garlic and sauté until soft.
While the mushrooms are cooking, combine eggs, light cream and a generous dash Tabasco in a small bowl. Mix well and add to the skillet.

Cook over medium high heat until the eggs have begun to set. Use a slotted spoon to carefully add the seafood. Stir to incorporate the seafood then add the wine and lemon juice.

Shake, tilt and work the pan. When egg mixture has set remove pan from heat. Place sliced tomatoes on top and sprinkle with goat cheese. Place pan in hot, 425° oven for 4 to 5 minutes. Allow to set for about 5 minutes. Remove frittata to plate. Top with a dollop of sour cream.

Chili Rellenos Casserole, Improved

This is a recipe that is absolutely loaded with fat from every source imaginable: eggs, lots of eggs; cheese, two different kinds and lots of each; and condensed milk. It is my fervent and completely unrealistic hope that the chilies absorb most of the calories. I don't know where I found this recipe. I have made it many times and it is always a hit. About two years ago, my daughter-in-law, Gabrielle took my recipe and improved it. It's a good thing she did, because I can't find the original.

      14 oz can of green chilies, drained, seeded, and rinsed
      ½ pound jack cheese, shredded
      ½ pound cheddar cheese, shredded
      4 eggs
      2 tablespoons all purpose flour
      1 large can evaporated milk

Line an 8 x10 or 9 x 12 baking pan with ½ the chilies. Cover the chilies with ½ of the jack and ½ of the cheddar cheese. Add a second layer of all the remaining chilies and repeat with the balance of the 2 cheeses. **Set aside.**

Use a small bowl to beat the eggs lightly. Add the flour and the evaporated milk to the beaten eggs and beat with an electric mixer until well blended. Pour the egg mixture over the cheese and chilies in the casserole dish. Bake for 40 minutes at 350° in a preheated oven.

Add Notes here...

16. VEGETABLES:

At home 5 vegetables were part of our daily fare. The first two, potatoes and iceberg lettuce were almost always served with dinner. The remaining trio: canned corn, canned peas and canned beans were all prepared in the same manner. They were heated, (boiled), salted and served with a touch of Imperial. I don't remember ever eating or even seeing green onions, radishes or sweet peppers.

Less common vegetables:

- Once a month we would have a boiled dinner; a meaty ham bone boiled with carrots, onions and cabbage.
- On rare occasions mom and dad would have asparagus. Even 50 years ago, asparagus was expensive and rarely in season. Larry, Sharon, Kathy and I thought asparagus looked weird, like a skinny tree, or a small forest of skinny little trees. Dad really liked it. He never encouraged us to try asparagus, and we never did. Dad was a smart, and rather ornery man.
- Mom liked cucumbers. Dad didn't. According to dad, the only reason God created cucumbers was so small children could make them into canoes.
- Tomatoes: Dad grew up on a farm. I'm sure fresh-farm vegetables were part of his diet. If so, he got over it.

Beyond the City Limits

He did like plants. We had lots of roses and other flowers, but we only grew one vegetable, the glorious tomato. Dad planted tomatoes along the side fence. They did well in that location. Mid-western summers are long, hot and humid. In the 1950's there was no air conditioning. We felt fortunate to have a fan, one fan. The point is we suffered through summer, but tomato plants thrived.

By July, we always had a bumper crop of ripe tomatoes with more coming every day. Dad liked tomatoes, but he was the only one who ate them. Actually, that's not true. Mom would eat a tomato slice or two with her salad.

My brother, Larry, really liked ripe tomatoes, but as ammunition, not food. He would sneak out to the tomato plants and load up his stash. Then he would take his position, like an enemy sniper, and lob overly ripe juicy red tomatoes at any poor soul, stupid enough to come within range.

I never ate tomatoes as a child. I wouldn't touch them and I tried very hard to keep them from touching me. I wasn't always successful. I can remember feeling smug on those rare occasions when I successfully avoided Larry and made it to the back door. Smug...Then, seemingly out of no where, SPLAT, Larry would paste me with a tomato, again.

I remember my first experience eating (rather than dodging) a tomato. It happened after I was out of high school. I ordered a hamburger in a restaurant and it came with a tomato slice that I failed to notice. I bit into the hamburger, blissfully unaware of any suspect tomato, and it was delicious! Today I love fresh ripe tomatoes and I like canned tomatoes as an off-season substitute.

A word or two about Vegetarians:

168

Andy Rooney says that vegetarian is an Indian word that means 'Lousy Hunter.' Many healthy people disagree. Some people, like my nieces Shelley and Cindy actually LIVE on vegetables by choice, not necessity. The vegetarian keys are a healthy attitude, fresh vegetables, and a lively imagination. I like lots of fresh vegetables but I am not ready to swear off meat.

Some Vegetable Secrets and Sins:

- Buy fresh, firm vegetables. Find a good green grocer who has reliably fresh produce. The stalls at Seattle's Pike Street Market are great. In Portland we have neighborhood fresh produce markets. They do not equal Pikes, but they are more convenient.

- In the summer, find your local Farmer's markets to take advantage of vegetables at the peak of the season. Make a point of asking how fresh is this? Where was this grown? When was it picked?

- Never, ever buy corn on the cob in a grocery store. Avoid buying fresh fruit or vegetables at a super market unless you are absolutely sure of the quality and freshness.

- If the vegetable is supposed to have a color, it should be bright, like bright red or green peppers, very yellow squash, white cauliflower, really green beans and red tomatoes.

- Plan ahead if you must, but don't buy too early, or in any great quantity. Be flexible. You can and should touch and even smell vegetables before purchase.

- You can try canning vegetables if you have absolutely nothing better to do with your time. However, before you get up to your elbows in pressure cookers and mason jars, think about it. Do you like canned vegetables? Would you buy them? If not, let someone else assume the role of Suzy Homemaker.

• Do not overcook vegetables, unless Ron Yasenchak is coming to dinner. Ron thinks that 'el dente' means undercooked. After all these years, it is time he learned the beauty of crunch.

• Some vegetables can be roasted or baked. Potatoes, asparagus, cauliflower, onions, garlic and certain squashes, are good examples.

• Most vegetables should be cooked quickly. Braise over low heat with a little butter. Or use a wok or a sauté pan and stir-fry the vegetables. I have a small plastic steamer from Magic Chef®. I use it to quickly microwave asparagus and broccoli. Here's the point: If the color of the vegetable has faded, the vegetable is overcooked.

Peppers:
There are a wide variety of peppers, green, red, yellow, orange, even purple that are available almost year round. There are dozens of ways to enjoy them: raw, in a salad; barely sautéed with chicken, beef or pork in a stir-fry or roasted. The green bell peppers are the most common but probably the least exciting. I like red and yellow peppers best. I think they add flavor, texture and color. Ron thinks that we have peppers, especially stir-fried peppers, way too often.

Onions:
Walla Walla, Washington is famous for Whitman College and big fat sweet onions. These are wonderful onions. Ron, Ronda and David all have sensitive stomachs and suffer greatly from the simple

pleasure of onions. However, they all can eat Walla Wallas without any problem. There is a down side to these marvelous onions: They are only available in June and July and they don't keep worth a darn. Fortunately the local markets have found some substitutes to tide onion lovers over for the rest of the year. These imported onions, Vidalia's, for example, are almost as good, but way too expensive. Green onions, leeks, and shallots are all examples of onion cousins that our family can live with. All are available year round. Lucky us.

These are some vegetables that I really like with my favorite ways to prepare them.

Asparagus:
This is absolutely my favorite vegetable. Asparagus is available in the Pacific NW nearly year round. Sometimes it is $5 a pound and sometimes it is $.79 a pound. I like it a lot. In late April through early June we have it at least 4 times a week. It's served raw, steamed, roasted, in a salad and stir-fried. I love it. Ron thinks we can and do have too much of a good thing. When he takes over the cooking he can make more menu decisions.

Some people prefer the skinny asparagus spears; others like the thicker ones. I don't think it makes much difference. When you cook asparagus, try to use roughly the same size spears; they will cook more evenly. In any case, buy fresh spears. Have your grocer help you. Wash them, then one at a time, snap off the tough ends where it breaks easily and throw them away. It's okay, you're rich.

Steamed: Sometimes the simplest method is best. I have a microwave steamer that is absolutely perfect for small amounts of asparagus. I place about ½ cup of water in the steamer and microwave for 1 minute. Then I place the spears in the steamer and return to the microwave for 2 to 3 minutes. They are barely done and bright green. I drain the water, add a little salt, pepper, and butter.

Cold: I like cooked asparagus in salads or as part of a relish tray. So I steam it, for a couple of minutes, drain it and plunge it into ice water to stop the cooking.

Broccoli:

Broccoli is a quality vegetable. It is inexpensive, available year round and loaded with vitamins, calcium and fiber. I buy and cook a lot of fresh broccoli. I use it in a few salads and in a lot of stir-fry dishes.

Ron is so sick of broccoli that he could puke.

- A lot of people use the broccoli heads and throw away the stalks. They are truly missing the best part. The end of the stalk is incredibly tough, but the middle part is really good.
- Wash the broccoli. Separate the head from the stalk. Cut off the last 2 inches of the stalk and discard. Peel the rest of the stalk. Slice it thinly in a diagonal, and use for stir fry. Broccoli cooks really fast. When it turns bright green, it is done.

Mushrooms:

Mushrooms thrive in dark, damp places. Is it any wonder that they do well in western Oregon? I think not. Commercial mushrooms, cremini, are always available. There is an active mushroom society in Portland. They can locate and accurately identify a huge number of edible mushrooms almost any time of year. The rest of us rely primarily on the marketplace. We once bought a log that had been seeded with shitake mushrooms spores. We grew them and ate them. They failed to reproduce. In the Northwest we have wild meadow, morels, and chanterelle mushrooms. They are all incredibly good.

Green Beans:

- I finally learned how to cook fresh green beans a couple of years ago. It is pretty simple.
- Buy fresh green beans at a farmers market
- Wash the beans and snip off the ends cut them in half if they are really long.
- Bring a large pot of salted water to a rolling boil.
- Boil the beans until they are tender, but still bright green, 6 to 10 minutes.
- Drain, add a little butter, salt and pepper and serve.

Brussels Sprouts:

My children called these 'fetal cabbages.' They have a point. Once in a great while I buy these. I wash them and peel off the tough outer leaves then I simmer them until they are tender in some chicken broth. They're pretty good, but it is hard to get past the feeling of infanticide.

Cabbage:

My mother made boiled dinner with a meaty ham bone, potatoes, carrots, onions and cabbage. She cooked it for a couple of hours or so. By that time, everything was tender and done. The cabbage and onions had completely disintegrated. It was filling, and it tasted okay. Dad loved it. He considered it a treat, so we had it pretty often. I only like cabbage 2 ways: sautéed with good German sausage, and in Ron's slaw.

Carrots:

This is another quality vegetable. In gourmet cooking, carrots are an important part of the 'trinity' used to sauté a lot of entrées. Their partners are celery and onions. Carrots don't really need all that much help. They are good raw. They add color, flavor and texture to stews, soups and pot roasts. They can be a welcome side dish.

This is one suggestion: Peel the carrots, slice on the diagonal. Steam in a little salted water until barely tender. Tip: add a pinch of sugar to the water. It helps bring out the flavor. Drain, sauté in a little butter with salt, pepper and fresh herbs. Serve.

Cauliflower:
Some vegetables are better raw than they are cooked. This could be one. I only like cooked cauliflower one way, in the microwave. *This is it:*
Prepare the cauliflower by washing it and removing most of the stem and bottom leaves. It is placed in a microwave dish.

- Add ½ cup water
- Cover the cauliflower with a lid or with plastic wrap.
- Microwave on high about 6 minutes. Test for doneness. If it is still rock hard, microwave for another minute or two.
- When the cauliflower is almost tender, drain, frost with mayonnaise and cover it with grated cheddar cheese. Return to the microwave for a minute or so until cheese is melted and mayonnaise is hot.

Celery:
Has there ever been a more worthless vegetable? I don't know. I buy celery by the stalk. I use it in the trinity and when I am really trying to lose weight. I suppose there are some perfectly good recipes for celery. You will have to find them on your own.

Corn:
All children love corn. I don't know if it's the color, the high sugar count or the fact that it is almost impossible to ruin. I like corn, and Connor, food critic extraordinary, loves it. My mother served canned corn, with salt. We loved it. We really loved corn on the cob. Mom cleaned it, removing all the silks and boiled it in salted

water for 12 to 15 minutes. That's the way most people still cook it. I have a better way.

Microwave Corn on the Cob:
"There is no finer way to cook corn than in the microwave oven." I heard that from Earl and Bobby, two good old boys teaching a class on microwave cooking. Strangely enough, they were right.

- Start with freshly picked corn. If it is more than a day old, it is not fresh.
- Remove some of the tough, nasty outer leaves, but do not strip the ear.
- Use a sharp knife and cut off the large end right at the crown.
- Place corn on a microwave dish in a spoke-like pattern with the fat ends sticking out. Microwave on high for 3 minutes per ear. I do 3 ears at a time; 9 minutes.
- Let corn rest and cool off a little.
- Grasp the silk ends and shake.
- The corn will emerge clean, silk-free and ready to eat.

Creamed corn is another story. It started with a can of creamed corn and a handful of breadcrumbs. Mom added a beaten egg, salt and an ounce of oleo. She topped with more breadcrumbs and baked until it was hot and bubbly. It was a regular staple at our house. I think I can live without it.

However, I found a corn soufflé recipe that is good. It calls for corn on the cob, but it can be made with purchased frozen corn. It is pretty darn good, more like a pudding than a soufflé.

Fresh Corn Soufflé

Ingredients:

6 ears fresh corn or about 2 pounds frozen, drained corn
(5 cups of corn)

4 TB butter (divided)	1¾ cup milk (divided)
1 tablespoon flour	½ cup chopped onion
2 large eggs	½ teaspoon salt and a pinch of
1 cup Panko	white pepper

Directions:

- Preheat oven to 350°
- Butter an 8 X 8 baking dish.
- Melt 1 tablespoon butter in a heavy medium saucepan over medium heat.
- Add flour, salt and pepper. Stir 2 minutes but do not brown.
- Gradually mix in ¾ cup milk. Bring to a boil, stirring constantly.
- Remove from heat and cool.
- In a separate bowl, whisk eggs and remaining 1cup milk. Whisk in 2/3 cup crackers, prepared corn mixture, remaining 3 cups corn and the onion.
- Transfer to prepared dish.
- Melt remaining 3 tablespoons butter in small, heavy skillet, add remaining crackers, toss with the butter. Sprinkle crumb on top corn mixture.
- Bake until knife inserted into center comes out clean, about 40 minutes.
- Serve immediately. This makes 8 side-dish servings.

Cucumbers:

In my opinion cucumbers are another limited value vegetable. However, Ron's mother made a cucumber salad that was truly inspired.

- She peeled the cucumber
- Cut it into super-thin slices
- Soaked it in salt water for about an hour.
- Drained the water and squeezed the cucumber slices to remove all moisture,
- And combined the slices with a mild vinegrette.

Lettuce:

There are lots of varieties of lettuce. I grew up with iceberg lettuce. It is available, but it lacks flavor, color, vitamins, nutrition and taste. Find something else. Tear or cut it into small enough pieces so you and your guests won't be biting off more than they can chew.

Sweet Garden Peppers:

I don't remember even seeing peppers as a kid. I am pretty sure I never ate them. Peppers are generally available and they are good. They come in a variety of colors from the common green to red, yellow and purple. Peppers add color, flavor and texture especially to stir fry dishes and salads. It is easy to roast whole sweet peppers and they are a wonderful addition to a sandwich. Peppers fit in the same general category as onions. You simply need to have them if you are going to assume the role of cook.

Tomatoes:

In Oregon we have wonderful, fresh local tomatoes for a very short period of time in late summer. The rest of the year, our tomato options are not all that great. The local grocery stores always have what they call fresh tomatoes. These off season placeholders are expensive. They rather look like a tomato, but they have no tomato smell or discernable taste. I call them plastic tomatoes, and I do not buy them. We eat canned tomatoes all winter, spring and most of every summer. I use them in vegetable salads as well as cooking. They're a little messy, but they smell and taste like real tomatoes because they are just that. Think about it. Canned tomatoes are packed at their peak of freshness.

Mushrooms:

If you don't like or eat mushrooms, you need to give them a chance. In the Northwest, there are dozens of wonderful mushrooms available in addition to the little button mushrooms in the local grocery stores. Try ordering a steak with shitake mushroom sauce on the side. I think you will find it close to great. Mushrooms are expensive, but they add so much flavor they're worth it. I have lots of mushroom recipes. Let me know when you get hooked and I will share.

Onions:

If you are going to cook, and be known as a cook, you need to keep onions in your kitchen. Fortunately, there are lots of onion options. Some people, like my husband and children, can't eat onions. Never fear. That's why God created shallots, and sweet onions. That's why supermarkets charge roughly ten times more per pound for the substitutes over the readily available cheap onions.

Peas:

Peas were a staple on Butrick Street. They came in a can. Mom heated them in a sauce pan and served with a generous dollop of Imperial Margarine. I don't buy canned peas, but I do buy and use frozen peas.

- A 2 pound bag of peas is almost perfect for a sprained ankle, or shoulder or back pain. If you look in my freezer, you can generally find a bag of peas inside a zip locked bag with a cautionary note: "Medicinal purposes only. Eat at your own peril." I make one creamed pea dish that is a tremendous hit with my age group.

Creamed Peas:
- Gently boil a package of peas in a small amount of water until just barely done. Drain off the water.
- Add about ½ tablespoons of flour to the peas. Stir gently, making sure the flour is well distributed.
- Add ½ cup milk or light cream, salt, pepper and parmesan cheese. Cook, stirring over medium low heat until sauce thickens. If sauce is too thick, add a little more milk. Season to taste and serve.

Potatoes: Potatoes are so versatile and extraordinary, they have their own section.

Root Vegetables: This recipe was originally part of a recipe for Pork Tenderloin and Root vegetables. Roasted vegetables are a real treat and this is where the recipe belongs.

Roasted Fresh Root Vegetables

2 medium potatoes
1 large sweet potato
2 large carrots
1 head garlic
1 onion
1 to 2 pounds of other vegetables of your choice such as turnips, parsnips
or beets
Olive oil
- Salt and pepper to taste

Preheat the oven to 400°. Peel and chop root vegetables into 1 inch pieces. Break up head of garlic, but do not peel the individual cloves. Place cut up vegetables and garlic in a roasting pan. Toss with olive oil to coat and season with salt and pepper. Roast vegetables in oven about 45 minutes until tender. Shake the roasting pan occasionally to brown vegetables on all sides.

Spinach:

This leafy, versatile, healthy vegetable has been elevated to a whole new level in the last few years. There are two things to remember about spinach:
- Spinach is grown in sandy soil, and it is hard to get all the sand off. Wash it carefully.
- It cooks in less than a minute. So be careful when you add it to a stir fry.
- For me, I like spinach a lot, but generally when I want a good spinach salad, I order it at a restaurant. Let them do the work!

Squash:

This is a generic term for a wide variety of vegetables. Squash has been given a pretty bad rap. Personally, I think it's the name. Squash. It rather sounds like something you should avoid. This is my recommendation: Avoid zucchini. Cut the others some slack.

- Acorn squash is great. Poke a few holes in it and bake it at 350° for about an hour. Cut it in half, scoop out the seeds, and serve it like a baked potato with salt, pepper and butter. Better yet, take it out a little early. Cut it in half, etc., and fill each half with Stouffers spinach soufflé. Return to oven for 20 minutes or so until soufflé is done. Oh my God. Die and go straight to heaven

- Butternut squash is really good. Cut it half, scoop out the seeds and bake it in serving sized pieces. It is firmer and meatier than acorn squash.
- Spaghetti Squash is the real winner. Think of it as fabulous fake, flavorful pasta. It is loaded with vitamins and it tastes good. We have it with marinara sauce, alone, or with a little parmesan cheese, salt, pepper and butter. Try it. You can find these in the fall of the year. They are pale yellow and kind of oblong. They are cooked whole, like an acorn squash. Bake squash until done, when a fork goes in easily and comes out clean. Cut in half, scoop out seeds, and then fluff up the squash.

Add vegetable recipes here...

17. DESSERTS

At my house dessert was our reward for finishing dinner. It is possible that everyone had dessert with every lunch and dinner, we certainly did. Dessert wasn't just an idea or suggestion, it was the law. Dad loved sweet stuff and Mom never met a desert she didn't like. You might say the crumbs didn't fall far from the fork; their children also loved desserts. Mom liked to bake. She was known for her pies, especially her tender, tasty pie crust. She also made cookies and several different cakes, like classic German Chocolate, from scratch.

Our Waukegan Desserts:
We had pie every Sunday, along with our Sunday fried chicken. Many of Mom's pies came out of a can. I remember cherry and apple pies that mom could and did make year round thanks to canned fruit filling. She also made wonderful raisin and pecan and lemon meringue pies. Mom would roll out any left over pie dough, sprinkle it with cinnamon and sugar and bake it. We called it cinnamon pie and we loved it. The secret to Mom's pies is the crust. This is her recipe. Mom got it from her brother, Elmer.

Elmer's Secret Recipe for Pie Crust

> 2 cups all purpose flour
> 1 cup solid shortening, (Mom used Crisco®)
> ¼ teaspoon salt
> 3 to 4 tablespoons of ice water

- Use a pastry cutter to blend the flour, salt and shortening together in a small bowl.
- Work the mixture until it is about the same texture as cornmeal.

- Cover the bowl and refrigerate for at least an hour and as long as a week.
- When you are ready to make the crust, place about half the dough in a small bowl.
- Add a small amount of ice water to the dough and blend in with a fork.
- Continue to add ice water until the dough just comes together like a ball.
- Roll out the crust on a flowered surface*. If the crust rips, or needs to be enlarged...

DO NOT RE-ROLL

Simply patch. This crust is light and flaky enough to easily accept the patch job. It will look good, but importantly it will taste great.

Note: Fresh pastry has a tendency to stick to whatever surface it touches. It also rips and tears very easily. I solved this problem by covering the rolling pin with a fabric sleeve and covering the surface with a well floured pastry cloth.

I never really understood the big mystery with piecrust. I suppose that's because I had the answer. Our whole family relied on Uncle Elmer's secret recipe...we still do. The only cousin that didn't know about it was Elmer's daughter, Marianne. She knows now. Up until 1995 when we shared Elmer's pie crust recipe with Marianne, she had to improvise. She came up with this recipe that is simply mixed together and patted into the pie pan. This is made with vegetable oil instead of solid shortening, so it is marginally healthier. It is also flaky and pretty darn good.

Marianne's No Roll – Pie Crust

1½ cups flour
1½ tablespoons sugar
¼ to ½ teaspoon salt
½ cup vegetable oil
2 tablespoons milk

Mix together the flour, sugar and salt, set aside. In a separate bowl, mix together the vegetable oil and milk. Add the milk mixture to the flour mixture and blend together with a fork. Transfer the dough to a pie pan and spread the mixture evenly over the bottom and up the sides of the pan. Forming a rim at the top. Fill the pie shell with your favorite pie filling and bake according to that recipe.

Mincemeat was Dad's favorite pie. Mom made it in the fall with fresh apples and other stuff. I found this hand-written spattered recipe in Mom's cookbook. I never, ever tasted Mom's mince meat. It didn't look or smell like anything I wanted to put in my mouth. My dad loved it, but he thought it was even better with venison. This is it:...

-Mabel's Mince Meat-

- A chunk of round steak, 2 to 2½ pounds, no gristle.
- Boil meat until tender in salted water
- Grind meat using the coarse blade of the food chopper
- Grind ½ pound suet and ½ pound oleo
- Grind apples using a ratio of 2 cups chopped apples to 1 cup chopped meat
- Add 1 pound raisins and the juice of 2 oranges
- Spices: Add 1 tablespoon cinnamon, 1 tablespoon mace, 1 teaspoon cloves.

- 1 tablespoon salt and teaspoon pepper.
- Add 1 pound brown sugar and 1 pound white sugar
- Add 2 cups hard cider or cranberry juice (I prefer cranberry juice)
- Cook slowly until it tastes like mince meat. I use strong coffee to thin it to proper consistency.
- Add in ¼ cup rum

Marianne's Custard Pie

1 unbaked 9 inch pie crust in a pie pan
4 slightly beaten eggs
½ cup granulated sugar
¼ teaspoon salt
1 teaspoon vanilla
2½ cups scalded milk

Preheat oven to 475°. Thoroughly mix the eggs with a whisk, add the sugar, salt and vanilla. Set aside. Bring the milk just to the boiling point and then slowly add the egg mixture whisking it briskly to prevent the eggs from cooking. Pour the mixture through a sieve into the pie shell. Place the pie in the oven and bake for 5 minutes. Reduce the oven temperature to 350° and continue to bake for another 18 to 20 minutes or until the pie is done. The custard will continue to cook as it sets.

This recipe makes a lovely smooth custard, but it is possible to ruin it. The following tips are offered by one who knows of what she speaks:

- If you whip the eggs instead of whisking them you will have bubbles on top of the finished custard. That is not good – it should be smooth.

- If you take the pie out of the oven before it is completely cooked, it will never, ever become custard.

Crumb Topped Apple Pie

This pie could and perhaps should be named 'Apple/Cheddar Custard Pie'. The apples, cheddar and sour cream give the pie distinction. The eggs turn it into custard. I don't remember where I found this recipe, but I have made it many times and it is surprisingly easy and reliably good. This is not like mom's apple pie. It's better.

> 9 inch unbaked pie shell
> 6 tablespoons butter, divided
> ¾ cup granulated sugar
> 1 cup sour cream
> ¾ cup flour, divided
> ¼ teaspoon salt
> 1 teaspoon vanilla
> 2 eggs
> 2 cups apples, thinly sliced
> ¾ cup shredded sharp cheddar cheese
> 1/3 cup brown sugar.

Use a mixer to combine the granulated sugar with 2 tablespoon of butter in a medium sized bowl. Add the sour cream, ¼ cup flour and salt, mix together, and then add the eggs and vanilla. Beat until all ingredients are evenly dispersed. Stir in the sliced apples and shredded cheese, and pour into the pie shell. Bake at 400° for 30 minutes.

While the pie is baking, combine the brown sugar, ½ cup flour and the remaining 4 tablespoons of butter in a small bowl. Mix the ingredients together with a pastry blender or a fork until it reaches a meal-like consistency.

Remove the pie from the oven and sprinkle the crumb mixture on top. Return the pie to the oven and continue to bake for 10 to 15 minutes longer or until the apples are tender.

COOKIES

We had three kinds of cookies at our house: chocolate chip, peanut butter and Spritz, which were only made at Christmas. When Grandma Aldridge visited, she made wonderful sugar cookies. Each basic recipe was doubled to make at least five dozen cookies. A batch of homemade cookies would last two or three days. The burned cookies would be the last to go. My brother Larry actually developed a taste for burned cookies and prefers them to this day. Mom made cookies twice a week and we never bought pre-packaged cookies, ever.

Chocolate Delights

I have no idea where I found this recipe. Bonanza was a popular television show a long time ago. On one episode, the character 'Hoss' made a mock apple pie out of crackers.

That episode spurred a whole bunch of recipes and that may be how I found this little gem. It is made with chocolate chips, or I never would have tried it. It also features soda crackers! The recipe is made in a blender and the finished cookies taste like little portable brownies.

  9 to 10 soda crackers
  ¾ cup walnuts
  1 – 6 ounce package chocolate chips

3 egg whites
1 cup powdered sugar
1 teaspoon vanilla

Preheat oven to 325°. Place 4 or 5 crackers in the blender and pulse until the crackers have been reduced to fine crumbs. Repeat the process with the rest of the crackers, then add the walnuts, and finally the chocolate chips. Pulse until all ingredients are finely chopped, then set aside. In a separate bowl, beat the egg whites until they form soft peaks, then add the powered sugar 2 tablespoons at a time. Continue to beat the eggs until they are stiff, but not dry. Fold in the crumbled mixture and the vanilla. Use a tablespoon to spoon the cookie mixture onto a baking sheet. Bake for 12 minutes. This recipe yields 3 dozen cookies.

Tom McCoy's Chocolate Chip Cookies

Tom is David's friend and one of my favorite people. He helped us build our garage at the A-Frame. He shared this recipe with me so I could bake his favorite cookie. This recipe makes at least four dozen large cookies. They disappeared so quickly I cannot provide an accurate yield.

2 eggs
¾ cup brown sugar
¾ cup granulated sugar
¾ cup real butter
1 teaspoon salt
1½ teaspoon vanilla
2½ cups flour
1 teaspoon baking soda
½ teaspoon salt
1 – 12 ounce package chocolate chips

Beat the eggs until light and frothy, set aside. In a separate bowl, blend the sugars with the butter then add the vanilla and the beaten eggs. Sift the dry ingredients together and add them slowly to the dough beating to incorporate all ingredients. Stir in the chocolate chips. Bake the cookies for 10 to 13 minutes in a 350° oven . Allow the cookies to set for a few minutes before removing them from the baking tin.

CAKES

Mom made cakes. When I was very little, all cakes were made from scratch. They were a rare and wonderful treat. In the early 1950's cake mixes were introduced. It meant we could have cake *far* more often. I don't remember asking God to bless Betty Crocker in my nightly prayers, but I could have. Betty Crocker was a permanent resident at our house. These are the cakes I remember, thanks to her and to General Mills®:

- Angel food cake with chocolate whipped cream frosting, my personal favorite
- Angel food cake with fresh strawberries, a close second
- Spice cake, Dad's favorite
- Chocolate cake with chocolate frosting, my brother, Larry's favorite
- Devil's food cake, just the name was enough to make it special
- Bringing up the rear, (in every sense of the phrase) was white cake (which was yellow) and marble cake.

My daughter Ronda makes beautiful, wonderful deserts. I can cook meals, and occasionally I tackle a dessert. The finished desserts usually taste pretty good, but they almost always look more than a little strange. 'Scary' is the descriptive term used by my daughter. The whole truth is that I am really not a very good baker.

Ronda explained my lack of success in this manner:

"It's like this: A recipe is a suggestion. You can add, subtract or change ingredients and it still turns out pretty good. Successful baking requires you to actually follow the recipe. It is more like a formula than a suggestion."

As it turns out I have dozens of dessert recipes – but I have only made a fraction of the total. I am including almost all of my tried and true dessert recipes. This just may be the shortest section in this book.

Caryl's Lemon Cake

This recipe is from Caryl Rivers. I worked with Caryl and her sister Janice at the IRS. Both ladies are very good cooks and each of them takes full credit for this recipe. The lemon cake is baked in a bundt pan and topped with a tart lemon glaze. The recipe is deceptively easy. It uses a lemon cake mix and unlike some of my dessert attempts, this recipe always works. One time when our daughter Ronda was about 13 years old, I left instructions for her to make this cake. Ronda followed the directions, but 15 or 20 minutes into the baking process, the oven caught fire. As I understand it, the element flamed brilliantly and then died forever.

I can't remember where I was, but Ronda called me in a panic. She explained the problem. I told her not to worry. I suggested she take the half-baked cake to one of our neighbors and use their oven to complete the cooking. And she did. In spite of its harsh treatment, the finished cake looked okay.

As God is my witness, I took that cake to a Bonsai luncheon/potluck at the beach. I was shocked and amazed when this dense, heavy cake was the hit of the luncheon. Everyone loved it and it disappeared almost immediately. I had to do a fast shuffle when asked for the recipe. Now, years later, I am happy to share it.

Ingredients:
1 package lemon cake mix
I small box lemon pudding
¾ cup vegetable oil
¾ cup orange juice
4 eggs
1 teaspoon fresh lemon juice
1 tablespoon grated lemon peel

Directions:
Combine the cake and pudding mix together in a large bowl. Add the oil, orange juice, eggs, lemon juice and grated lemon peel and beat well with an electric mixer. ***Set aside.***

Oil and lightly flour a Teflon coated bunt pan. Be sure to shake off any excess flour. Pour the cake batter into the bunt pan. Before placing the cake in the oven, run a knife all around to break air pockets, then lift up cake and let it drop back down. Bake this cake at 350° for 50 to 55 minutes or until done.

Lemon Glaze

1 cup powered sugar
1 to 2 tablespoons fresh lemon juice
zest from 1 fresh lemon

Combine the powered sugar and lemon juice. Stir to dissolve any lumps then add the lemon zest. Stir, adjusting the amount of lemon and sugar until the glaze is smooth and light in consistency.

Allow the cake to sit for a half hour or so in the pan, then turn the cake onto a serving dish. Top the lemon cake with the glaze while the cake it still warm.

Chocolate Pumpkin Cake

This is a recipe that Sharon and I adapted from a recipe for zucchini bread. We had to substitute something for zuchinni when Sharon's crop failed. We chose canned pumpkin. This is a very heavy moist cake that is cooked for a long time in a bunt pan. This cake doesn't need any kind of frosting, however it is wonderful with vanilla ice cream.

Ingredients:
3 eggs, well beaten
1½ cups granulated sugar
½ cup brown sugar
3 teaspoons vanilla
1 cup vegetable oil
2 cups canned pumpkin (or shredded zucchini)
3 cups flour
½ cup cocoa
¼ teaspoon baking powder
1 teaspoon salt
1 teaspoon baking soda
3 teaspoons cinnamon
1 cup chopped walnuts
1 - 6 ounce package of chocolate chips

Preheat the oven to 350°. Prepare the baking pan by spraying it with a vegetable spray and then dusting the pan with flour. Be sure to shake off any excess. Beat the eggs until light and fluffy then add the sugars, vanilla and pumpkin. Beat the mixture to combine thoroughly. Sift the dry ingredients together and gradually add them to the batter. Stir in the chocolate chips and the chopped nuts. Pour the mixture into the prepared bundt pan and bake for 50 to 60 minutes or until an inserted toothpick comes out clean. Allow the cake to rest for at least an hour and then turn it onto a serving dish.

Dump Cake
When our children were little, everyone I knew made some version of this cake. Ronda and David loved to 'make this cake' when they were very little. I would prepare the baking pan and measure all the ingredients. David would dump them in and Ronda would stir everything together. The ingredients are undeniably weird, but the cake is either surprisingly tasty or good enough for little children especially when they can brag, I made it 'all by myself!'

> 3 cups flour
> 2 cups sugar
> 6 tablespoons unsweetened cocoa
> 2 teaspoons baking soda
> 1 teaspoon salt
> 2 tablespoons white vinegar
> ¾ cup cooking oil
> 2 cups water

optional ingredients:
- ½ cup chopped nuts
- 1 small package of semi sweet chocolate chips

Preheat the oven to 350°. Grease an 8 inch baking pan (or spray with a non-stick coating). Add all of the ingredients to the pan in the order given, mix thoroughly and bake for 30 minutes.

Puddings and Custards

At home we had chocolate, vanilla and butterscotch pudding. All of these puddings came from a box. The dried pudding mix was combined with milk and cooked on top the stove. More times than not, the puddings burned or at least got scorched. Mom was easily distracted and she didn't have the best cookware. I have discovered it is a lot easier to make puddings and custards if one has the time to cook the pudding slowly, stir it often and use a heavy bottomed saucepan.

Easy Lemon Curd

My friend Janet Kent has a sister named Joyce who lives in Palm Springs. Joyce has a Meyer's Lemon Tree in her Palm Springs landscape. When Joyce comes to Portland, she brings a lot of fresh lemons, and Jan uses them to make this dessert.

¼ cup cornstarch
1 cup sugar
2 cups lemon juice*
2 tablespoons lemon zest
2 tablespoons butter
2 eggs
¼ cup sugar
• dash of salt
1-9 inch pie shell, baked

Mix cornstarch and sugar in a heavy bottomed saucepan. Add the lemon juice and zest, stirring to combine all ingredients. Place saucepan over medium high heat. Cook, stirring frequently, until the mixture is thick and clear. Add butter to the mixture and remove from the heat, and set it aside.

Beat the eggs, salt and sugar together in a medium sized bowl until the mixture is semi-thick. Pour part of the hot custard mixture into the egg mixture and combine well. Add the rest of the hot custard and blend thoroughly. *Refrigerate until firm.*

Joyce has adapted this recipe to require less sugar than a traditional lemon curd. Consequently, she does not use 2 full cups of the Meyer's lemons juice even though they are less tart than the yellow varieties available in our local markets. She uses 1½ cups fresh lemon juice and ½ cup of water. If she uses yellow lemons, the ratio of fresh juice to water is equal, a cup of each.

Another note from Joyce: Eggbeaters® work just fine in the curd. You can also cook the lemon mixture in the microwave. I think it's less hassle and quicker on top of the stove since you have to open the microwave and stir every couple of minutes.

Joyce offers the following suggestions for serving this lemon curd:

- Flavor plain yogurt with the curd
- Spread it like jam on toast or English muffins
- Pour it into a baked 9 inch pie shell
- Serve with Dutch Baby Pancakes

The Last Word

Thank you for the privilege of sharing my recipes and family stories with you.

***Beyond the City Limits** is a step back in time.*

I hope you'll try the recipes, well, maybe not all the recipes.

I enjoyed sharing family stories with you.

Now it is time to get cooking!